THE NO TIME TO COOK! BOOK

THE NO TIME TO COOK! BOOK

100 MODERN, SIMPLE RECIPES
IN 20 MINUTES OR LESS

Elena Rosemond-Hoerr

Penguin Random House

US Editors Christy Lusiak, Allison Singer
US Consultant Kate Ramos
Senior Editor Bob Bridle
Designer Harriet Yeomans
Editorial Assistant Alice Kewellhampton
Design Assistant Laura Buscemi
Managing Editor Dawn Henderson
Managing Art Editor Christine Keilty
Senior Jacket Creative Nicola Powling
Jacket Art Editor Kathryn Wilding
Pre-Production Producer Andy Hilliard
Senior Producer Jen Scothern
Deputy Art Director Maxine Pedliham
Art Director Peter Luff
Publisher Peggy Vance

Additional contributor
Laura Herring

Studio photography
Stuart West and William Reavell

First American Edition, 2015
Published in the United States by
DK Publishing, 345 Hudson Street,
New York, New York 10014

Copyright © 2015
Dorling Kindersley Limited
A Penguin Random House Company

10 9 8 7 6 5 4 3 2 1
001—259427—Apr/2015

Published in Great Britain by Dorling
Kindersley Limited

A catalog record for this book is available
from the Library of Congress.
ISBN 978-1-4654-2990-2

DK books are available at special discounts
when purchased in bulk for sales promotions,
premiums, fundraising, or educational use.
For details, contact: DK Publishing Special
Markets, 345 Hudson Street, New York, New
York 10014 SpecialSales@dk.com.

Color reproduction by AltaImage
Printed and bound in China

All images © Dorling Kindersley Limited
For further information see:
www.dkimages.com

A WORLD OF IDEAS:
SEE ALL THERE IS TO KNOW

CONTENTS

FOREWORD

I am, above all else, a lover of food. I cherish the simple act of creating a delicious, nourishing meal and feeding it to those that I love. It is the greatest gift that I can give, and I love giving it. However, this lofty sentiment is much easier to keep in my heart and mind on Sunday afternoon baking bread in the dusky sunlight of my kitchen than on a Tuesday night, tired and spent from a long day at work. In those moments, I sometimes think that perhaps I am a lover of takeout Indian food above all else. More often than not, I find myself desperate for any tip or trick that can help me conjure up a healthy and delicious home-cooked meal that, if the stars align, can be on my dinner table quickly and effortlessly.

I am not alone in this journey. Friends and family alike confess to me their struggles with coming up with creative, affordable, and time-efficient options for meal times. I can't tell you how many times I've found myself agreeing as someone talked about the importance of meal prep, of stocking your pantry with essentials, and of short cuts that save on time but don't sacrifice quality. It was these conversations that were in my mind when we began working on *The No Time to Cook Book*. We set out to make a book that would give readers access to not only hundreds of recipes, but also techniques, tips, and foundational ideas that they could adapt and make their own. Teach a man to fish, as they say.

The No Time to Cook Book presents recipes in a way that is visually engaging, offering step-by-step illustrations, infographics, and mix-and-match flavor ideas that will excite the mind and make you think about cooking in different ways. Each page is designed to inspire.

The book begins with a section full of practical ideas to set you up for quick cooking, such as equipment and pantry essentials, how to prepare some key ingredients quickly and efficiently, and 20 of the best time-saving tips around.

The recipes that follow are organized by meals, with suggestions for each time of the day, allowing you to incorporate 20-minute recipes and quick-cook tips into every aspect of your life—from an on-the-go breakfast to a last-minute dinner party. And the recipes, whose ingredients, style, and cooking techniques draw inspiration from global traditions and trends, offer something for everyone.

You have at your fingertips a wealth of recipes and ideas that will help you navigate the daily task of providing yourself and the people you love with wholesome, delicious, and—equally as important—quick-to-prepare foods.

Elena Rosemond-Hoerr

ESSENTIAL EQUIPMENT

Investing in a few basic pieces of kitchen equipment will mean you always have the right tool for the job. This will save you time when preparing and cooking your food, and make spending time in the kitchen a pleasure.

It's also important to organize your equipment and ingredients (see pp12–15) so that you always know where to find things—your time is best spent making delicious food, not hunting for an elusive frying pan or jar of mayonnaise!

Keep your saucepans stacked by size, your utensils in easy reach, and your pantry, fridge, and freezer tidily stocked. Turn cans and jars so that the labels are clearly visible and facing outward, and when labeling your own food, be sure to use permanent marker, which won't rub off.

WOODEN SPOON

A trusty wooden spoon, for stirring and beating, is durable and won't scratch your pots and pans.

FRYING PAN

Buy one that is large enough to cook an omelet. A frying pan with a lid is helpful to speed up cooking.

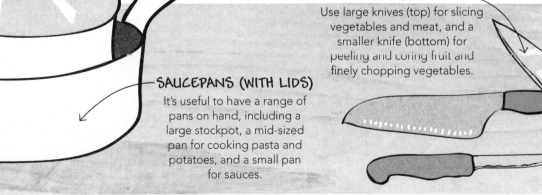

SHARP KNIVES

Use large knives (top) for slicing vegetables and meat, and a smaller knife (bottom) for peeling and coring fruit and finely chopping vegetables.

SAUCEPANS (WITH LIDS)

It's useful to have a range of pans on hand, including a large stockpot, a mid-sized pan for cooking pasta and potatoes, and a small pan for sauces.

SPEED PEELER

This can also be used to ribbon vegetables for quick salads and stir-fries.

GRATER

For grating, shredding, shaving, and zesting. Look for one with a sturdy handle.

MEASURING CUP

You need one with a wide spout for easy pouring and a good-sized handle.

POTATO MASHER

A curved head will let you mash right to the edges of bowls and pots.

COLANDER

As well as for rinsing and draining, this can double as a steamer.

CAN OPENER

This should be comfortable to hold and latch onto the can easily.

GARLIC CRUSHER

Saves you time when preparing garlic, and can even be used with unpeeled cloves.

BLENDER

A pitcher-style blender makes quick work of sauces, soups, and smoothies.

MIXING BOWL

For mixing dry and wet ingredients. One with a spout makes it easy to pour batters.

CUTTING BOARDS

You'll need two good boards—one for veggies and one for meat. Buy them in different colors so you remember which is which.

BAKING SHEET

One with a rim or lip will help prevent spillages.

SMART SHOPPING

Aim to do a big shop every couple of weeks to replenish your pantry ingredients, then stock up on fresh items in between. This will allow you to produce quick, delicious meals using the core ingredients on your shelves. See below for key pantry ingredients and pages 14–15 for your fridge and freezer essentials.

PANTRY ESSENTIALS

CANS

- **Chopped tomatoes** – for quick pasta sauces and to bulk up leftovers.
- **Beans** (such as black, kidney, and navy) – add to soups and stews for extra texture, fiber, and protein.
- **Chickpeas** – add to salads, stews, and curries, or use to make hummus.
- **Coconut milk** – use in noodle soups and curries.
- **Salmon, tuna, and crab** – use in pasta sauces, salads, wraps, tarts, and fishcakes.
- **Fruit** (such as peaches or pineapple pieces) – for smoothies, tarts, and pies.

JARS

- **Sun-dried tomatoes**, artichoke hearts, and roasted red bell peppers – use on pizzas, in salads, and as part of a mezze.
- **Pesto** – use as a pasta sauce, to add flavor to dressings, and mixed into mayo as a dip or spread.

DRIED GOODS

- **Pasta** – the ultimate quick-cook standby.
- **Rice noodles** – use in soups, stir-fries, and salads.
- **Instant rice** – as a side and in risottos and salads.
- **Bulgur wheat** – as a side or in a salad.
- **Couscous** – as a side for curries and stews, or use in salads.
- **Oats** – for oatmeal and granola; or use in bars and cookies.
- **All-purpose flour** – for pastries, cookies, cakes, and quick white sauces.
- **Sugar** – add a teaspoon to tomato sauce for extra flavor.
- **Good-quality bouillon cubes** – as a base for soups and to add flavor to stews.
- **Mixed nuts and dried fruits** – to top oats and yogurt, or to use in cookie dough, salads, and curries.
- **Wraps and tortillas** – for fajitas, lunch wraps, and as a quick pizza base.

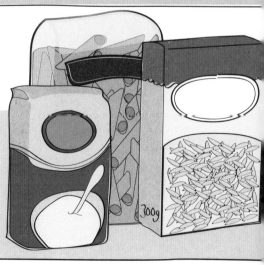

SAUCES AND PASTES

- **Harissa** – use in sauces and with meatballs, or mix with mayo as a dip.
- **Tomato paste** – add to tomato sauces for richness.
- **Mayonnaise** – flavor with herbs, harissa, or lemon juice for dressings; mix with garlic, pesto, or harissa as a dip or spread.
- **Worcestershire sauce** – add to meat-based dishes for extra flavor; sprinkle over cheese on toast.
- **Tabasco sauce** – add a few drops for instant heat.
- **Soy sauce** – use in stir-fries, noodle soups, and as a dip.
- **Good-quality curry paste** – for quick curries, and to pour over meat or fish as an instant marinade.

ON YOUR WINDOW SILL

Fresh, growing herbs, such as parsley, basil, mint, and thyme, add flavor during cooking, and are perfect as a garnish, torn into salads, or as part of a filling for sandwiches and wraps.

OILS AND VINEGARS

- **Olive oil** – for general cooking.
- **Extra-virgin olive oil** – for dressings and dips, and for drizzling.
- **Vegetable or sunflower oil** – for frying at high temperatures.
- **Balsamic vinegar** – for dressings and dips, and for adding sweetness to tomato sauces.
- **Red or white wine vinegar** – add to stews, soups, and sauces to elevate the flavors.

DRIED HERBS AND SPICES

- **Red pepper flakes** – sprinkle over soups and use in stews and sauces.
- **Bay leaves** – add to rice and stews for extra flavor.
- **Ground cinnamon** – sprinkle over breakfast oatmeal, add to stews, and use in cookies and cakes.
- **Cayenne pepper** – use as a milder, warmer alternative to black pepper.
- **Ground coriander** – add to curries and tomato sauces.
- **Ground ginger** – add to curries and sauces; use instead of fresh ginger in stir-fries.

- **Mixed Italian herbs** – use in sauces or scatter over fish or chicken before cooking.
- **Salt and black peppercorns** – for seasoning most dishes.

Good buys
Look out for ingredients that will save you precious minutes, such as instant rice, fresh pasta, and even pre-washed salads.

CONTINUED

IN THE FRIDGE

FRESH SALAD AND GREEN VEGGIES

Use in entrée salads and side salads, add to stir-fries, or serve alongside simply cooked meat or fish.

EGGS

Endlessly versatile for quick cooking.

YOGURT

Serve with berries and oats for an instant breakfast, add to smoothies, or use as an accompaniment to spicy foods. Thin down and flavor with pesto, harissa, or lemon juice to use as a dressing.

IN THE FREEZER

FROZEN PEAS

Add to quick soups and stews, mix into fishcakes or tart fillings, or use as a simple side dish with flavored butter melted over the top.

FROZEN VEGETABLES

Broccoli florets, fava beans, and carrots are all great standby items for stir-fries, soups, stews, and as side dishes.

INDIVIDUAL FISH FILLETS

Freeze white fish and salmon fillets in a sealable freezer bag with slices of lemon or halved cherry tomatoes, chopped fresh ginger and soy sauce, or just a little butter and salt and pepper. Then simply defrost overnight and pan-fry in butter.

BREAD

Slice and freeze leftover bread. Then, use the frozen slices to make sandwiches—they will defrost in time for lunch.

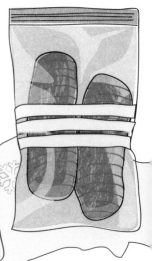

MUSTARD

Spread over steaks before cooking, combine with olive oil to make a quick dressing, or mix with mayo and use in sandwiches and salads.

OLIVES

Add to salads and sauces, use as a topping for pizzas, and include as part of a mezze.

BUTTER

For general cooking and to add richness to risottos. Also, flavor with herbs, garlic, or red pepper flakes and melt over steaks, rice, or cooked vegetables.

Bulk-buy deals

Take advantage of any bulk-buy deals or price reductions on multi-packs. You may not need several packages of ground beef or chicken breasts now, but freeze them individually and you'll be set for several meals to come.

BACON

Chop and cook with onions as the base for a tomato sauce, or fry until crispy and scatter over salads for a quick flavor hit.

CHICKEN PORTIONS

Chicken breasts, thighs, and drumsticks are extremely versatile and quick to cook. (Always make sure they are thoroughly defrosted before cooking.)

GROUND MEAT

Use for meatballs, burgers, and quick pasta sauces.

STOCK

Use as the base for soups, noodle broths, and to add flavor to stews or when cooking rice or couscous.

MIXED BERRIES

Use in smoothies, with breakfast oats and yogurt, or in desserts.

READY-TO-ROLL PUFF PASTRY

Perfect for making quick pies and tarts.

SPEEDY SKILLS MASTERCLASS

DICING AN ONION

1 Chop off each end of the onion—the root and tip.

2 Rest a flat end on the cutting board and cut the onion in half.

3 Peel the skin off of one half and rest the flat side on the board with the cut ends facing left and right in front of you.

PREPARING A BELL PEPPER

1 Slice off the top and bottom of the pepper.

2 Pull out the seeds and white membrane.

3 Cut the pepper in half from top to bottom.

PREPARING AN AVOCADO

1 Carefully slice all the way around the avocado through to the pit.

2 Holding the avocado in the palm of your hand, use your other hand to twist the top half of the avocado to separate the halves.

CHOPPING HERBS

1 Strip the leaves from the stems and gather them in a tight pile.

2 Slice through the herbs, holding them together with your other hand.

CHOPPING GARLIC

1 Use the flat edge of a large knife blade and pound the garlic clove, pressing down with your palm.

You may not be able to chop vegetables as fast as a professional chef (who has, after all, been practicing for years), but here are some top tips to help you on your way. Use a sharp knife and start off slowly until you gain confidence.

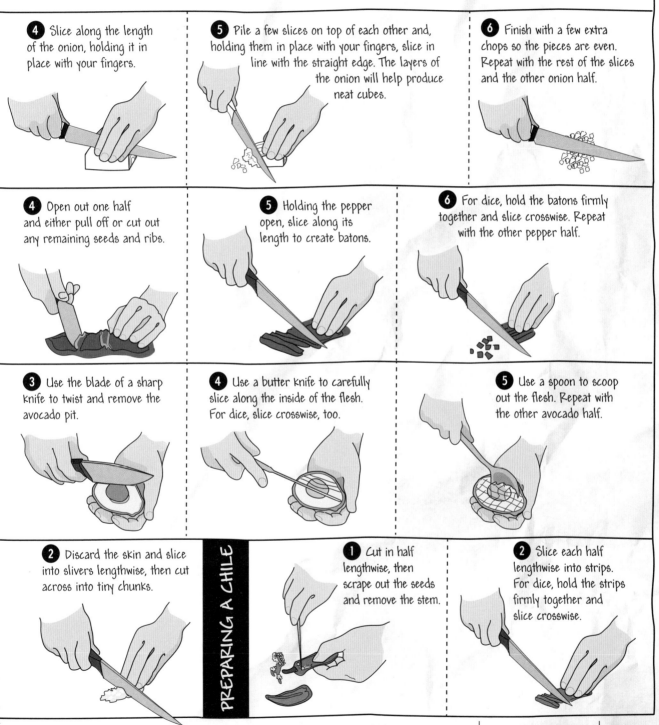

4 Slice along the length of the onion, holding it in place with your fingers.

5 Pile a few slices on top of each other and, holding them in place with your fingers, slice in line with the straight edge. The layers of the onion will help produce neat cubes.

6 Finish with a few extra chops so the pieces are even. Repeat with the rest of the slices and the other onion half.

4 Open out one half and either pull off or cut out any remaining seeds and ribs.

5 Holding the pepper open, slice along its length to create batons.

6 For dice, hold the batons firmly together and slice crosswise. Repeat with the other pepper half.

3 Use the blade of a sharp knife to twist and remove the avocado pit.

4 Use a butter knife to carefully slice along the inside of the flesh. For dice, slice crosswise, too.

5 Use a spoon to scoop out the flesh. Repeat with the other avocado half.

2 Discard the skin and slice into slivers lengthwise, then cut across into tiny chunks.

PREPARING A CHILE

1 Cut in half lengthwise, then scrape out the seeds and remove the stem.

2 Slice each half lengthwise into strips. For dice, hold the strips firmly together and slice crosswise.

20 TIME-SAVING TIPS

① FLAVOR HITS

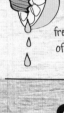

Add instant flavor with some simple ingredients. A squeeze of lemon juice, scattering of zest, splash of chili sauce, or some freshly chopped herbs all add lots of flavor with very little effort.

② SCRUB UP

When you come home from grocery shopping, wash fresh produce before putting it away. That way you won't have to scrub it clean when you're pressed for time making dinner.

③ THE NIGHT BEFORE...

Take meat or fish out of the freezer and let it defrost in the fridge overnight. Also, check that you have everything you need—you can pick up any last-minute items on your way home from work the next day.

④ FREEZER MARINADES

Combine pieces of meat with marinade ingredients (see pp198–9), seal in a plastic bag, then pop them in the freezer. When you defrost the meat, it will be flavored and ready to cook.

⑤ FLAVORED BUTTERS

Finely chop leftover herbs, mix with softened butter, and freeze. You can then slice off rounds and use while cooking for an herby flavor hit (add to the pan when cooking steak, melt over vegetables or rice, or toss through fresh pasta).

⑥ WAYS WITH ICE-CUBE TRAYS

Freeze any leftover wine in an ice-cube tray. This saves you having to open a fresh bottle just to add a splash when cooking. You can also freeze cubes of stock and fresh herbs in olive oil for instant flavor.

⑦ IT'S A BREEZE IF YOU FREEZE

Make a big batch of your favorite meal and freeze leftovers in individual portions. That way you'll have dinner ready at a moment's notice. You can do the same for sweets—just make individual desserts in ramekins, and freeze.

⑧ LITTLE HELPERS

You don't want too many cooks in the kitchen... but a helping hand goes a long way! Why not enlist a friendly sous chef to chop, stir, and help clean up as you go?

⑨ INSTANT SNACKS

Worried that there's nothing for your guests to nibble on? Simply skewer a selection of olives, anchovies, cheeses, hams, cherry tomatoes, sun-dried tomatoes—or any other tasty morsels you have in the pantry or fridge!

⑩ GET TO KNOW YOUR RECIPE

Read the recipe all the way through before you start. Knowing exactly what you need to do, and the right order to do it in, will save you time and avoid any surprises once you get going.

⑪ BE FLEXIBLE

Don't worry if you don't have a particular ingredient. Rather than spending time looking for an alternative recipe, just swap the ingredient for something similar.

Here are our top 20 tips for the time-pressed cook. There's advice about ways of getting ahead before you start, tricks for cutting down the time you spend preparing and cooking your food, ingenious ways to add instant flavor and interest to your meals, and much more.

12 BE PREPARED

Weigh, measure, and prep your ingredients first. This will prevent any delays when you suddenly have to juice a lemon or seed a chile, say, when you're meant to be stirring a sauce.

13 COOK ONCE, EAT TWICE

Once you're in the kitchen, apron on, it doesn't take much extra effort to prepare two dishes at the same time. While your oven is heating up tonight's pork chops, why not pop in a couple of chicken breasts on a separate pan? You will save money on your energy bill and be well on the way to tomorrow's dinner.

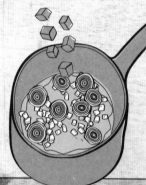

14 CHOP, CHOP!

Don't just chop one onion, chop two while you're at it! Then, freeze the second one in a sealed freezer bag for another time (the same applies to most chopped veggies and herbs). When you're ready to use it, just pour the frozen vegetable straight into the pan.

15 SIZE MATTERS

Chop your meat or veggies into small pieces to reduce the cooking time. Equally, thinner-cut steaks, or thicker pieces of meat that have been flattened, will cook very quickly.

16 COOKING METHODS

Pan-frying, grilling, broiling, and stir-frying are much quicker than baking in the oven or slowly simmering on the stove. Lean cuts of meat and leafy vegetables, for example, only require a quick pan-fry or steam.

17 YOUR FAVORITE CUP

Rather than weighing out rice, pasta, or other dried goods each time, find a cup or mug that holds the perfect portion size and use that instead. Also, learn to recognize what a tablespoon of oil looks like in the pan so you can simply swirl it in.

18 GET STARTED

Before you do anything else, boil some water and preheat the oven (if needed). As soon as the recipe calls for boiling water or for something to be popped in the oven, you'll be ready to go in an instant.

20 KEEP IT CLEAN

Cooking a meal in 20 minutes is fantastic; spending the next hour cleaning up, less so! As you go along, put any waste in the garbage, rinse the cutting board, and wipe the worktop. That way you'll just be left with a small amount of cleaning up.

19 DON'T PLATE UP

Save time when serving by placing large sharing platters in the middle of the table. It's quicker than plating up individual portions and creates a relaxed, sharing atmosphere.

SPEEDY BREAKFAST AND BRUNCH

SPEEDY SUMMER FRUIT SALAD

10 MINS OR LESS!

Dressing this fruit salad in a refreshing lemon and mint syrup helps the fruit stay fresh and colorful, and tastes delicious too! This is lovely for a light breakfast—add a dollop of yogurt if you want something a little more filling.

SERVES 4-6 • **READY IN** 5 mins

1 MAKE THE SYRUP

Put the sugar, lemon juice, and 2 tablespoons of water in a small, heavy-bottomed saucepan, place over low heat, and heat gently until the sugar melts. Cool, then stir in the mint.

2 MIX IT ALL UP

Mix all the fruit together in a bowl and toss it with the syrup. Chill until required, or eat immediately.

TIP – Use any combination of fruits, but try to avoid bananas or really ripe raspberries, which will disintegrate when mixed with the other fruit.

PLAN OF ACTION!

1 MAKE SYRUP ⟶ **2** MIX IT UP

INGREDIENTS

2 tbsp superfine sugar

juice of ½ lemon

2 tbsp finely chopped mint leaves

½ small cantaloupe, peeled, seeded, and cut into ½in (1cm) cubes

3½oz (100g) strawberries, halved or quartered, depending on size

1¾oz (50g) blueberries

1¾oz (50g) green, seedless grapes, halved

2 kiwi fruit, peeled and cut into ½in (1cm) cubes

WHEEL OF SMOOTHIES

What better way to start your day than with a delicious hit of vitamins and energy from a speedy smoothie? This wheel presents hundreds of exciting combinations— use it to inspire your next tasty blend.

MAKE YOUR SMOOTHIE

Use the ingredient suggestions as a guide, then adjust to taste. So if you want to use two liquids or no veggies, for example, that's fine! The quantities are for 1 serving.

- - - - - - - - - - - - - - - - - - -

① CHOOSE YOUR LIQUID
Add it to the blender.

② ADD A THICKENER
If you want a more substantial smoothie.

③ POP IN SOME VEGGIES
Such as leafy greens or summer squashes.

④ ADD YOUR FRUITY INGREDIENT
Or make fruit the star of the show.

⑤ THROW IN THE EXTRAS
Add your choice of flavorings and garnishes.

⑥ BLEND IT ALL UP
Blend to your desired consistency. Serve in a glass or pour into a bottle to drink on the go.

Start small
with the flavorings—
then taste your
smoothie and add
more, if you like.

① LIQUIDS

GREEN TEA
⅔ cup, cooled

FRUIT JUICE
⅔ cup

COCONUT MILK
¼ cup + ½ cup water

MILK
⅔ cup, dairy or dairy-free

COCONUT WATER
⅔ cup

YOGURT
2 tbsp, flavored or plain

⑤ FLAVORINGS AND GARNISHES

HEMP SEEDS
1 tbsp

POMEGRANATE
seeds from ½ fruit

DATES
handful, pits removed

HONEY OR MAPLE SYRUP
1 tsp

VANILLA EXTRACT
½ tsp

GRAHAM CRACKER
x 1, crumbled

COCOA POWDER
1 tbsp

GROUND NUTMEG
½ tsp

GROUND CINNAMON
½ tsp

CAYENNE PEPPER
½ tsp

CARDAMOM
seeds from 1 pod, crushed

GINGER
thumb-sized piece, peeled and grated

LEMON OR LIME
juice of ¼ fruit

FRESH MINT
small handful, chopped

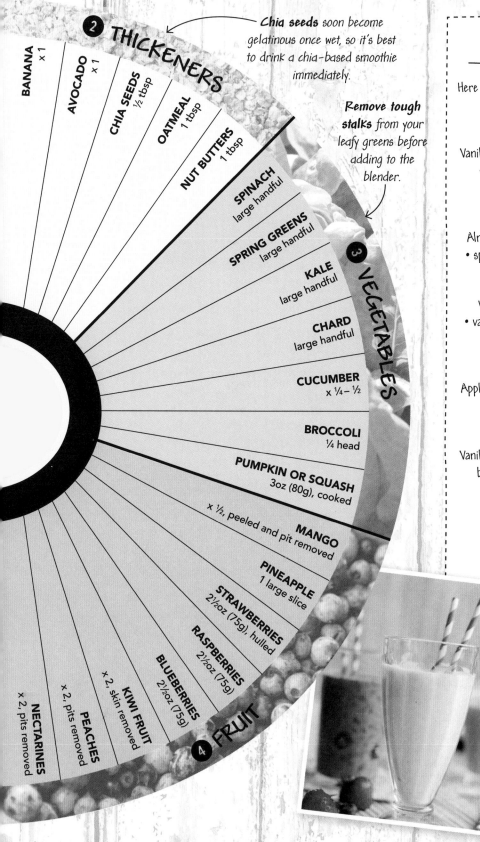

2 THICKENERS

BANANA
x 1

AVOCADO
x 1

CHIA SEEDS
½ tbsp

OATMEAL
1 tbsp

NUT BUTTERS
1 tbsp

Chia seeds soon become gelatinous once wet, so it's best to drink a chia-based smoothie immediately.

Remove tough stalks from your leafy greens before adding to the blender.

3 VEGETABLES

SPINACH
large handful

SPRING GREENS
large handful

KALE
large handful

CHARD
large handful

CUCUMBER
x ¼ – ½

BROCCOLI
¼ head

PUMPKIN OR SQUASH
3oz (80g), cooked

4 FRUIT

MANGO
x ½, peeled and pit removed

PINEAPPLE
1 large slice

STRAWBERRIES
2½oz (75g), hulled

RASPBERRIES
2½oz (75g)

BLUEBERRIES
2½oz (75g)

KIWI FRUIT
x 2, skin removed

PEACHES
x 2, pits removed

NECTARINES
x 2, pits removed

TOP COMBOS

Here are a few of our favorite smoothie ideas, to get you started...

DREAMY PEACH

Vanilla yogurt • banana • strawberries • peaches • ground cinnamon • mint leaves

GREEN POWER

Almond or coconut milk • avocado • spinach • hemp seeds • lime juice

PUMPKIN PIE

Whole milk • cooked pumpkin • vanilla extract • ground cinnamon • crumbled graham cracker

JADE

Apple juice • cucumber • lemon juice • honey • mint leaves

NUTTY BLUE

Vanilla yogurt • milk • smooth peanut butter • blueberries • peaches • vanilla extract

TROPICAL BREAKFAST SMOOTHIE

This quick and healthy smoothie uses frozen mango, which means the only preparation you have to do is peel and slice the bananas! For a creamier drink, use whole milk instead of apple juice.

SERVES 2 • **READY IN** 5 mins
SPECIAL EQUIPMENT Blender or hand-held blender

INGREDIENTS

- 1 banana, peeled and sliced
- 3½oz (100g) frozen mango cubes
- ¼ cup Greek yogurt
- 1½ tbsp honey
- 1 cup apple juice
- ice cubes, to serve (optional)

1 BLEND THE INGREDIENTS
Place all the ingredients except the ice cubes in a blender and process until you have a thick, smooth drink, or blend them with a hand-held blender.

2 SERVE WITH ICE (IF YOU LIKE)
Pour the smoothie into glasses to serve immediately. Add ice cubes if you like, or if it is a particularly hot day.

Try adding
2 tbsp rolled oats to the smoothie mix before blending for a filling "breakfast in a glass."

PLAN OF ACTION!
1 BLEND THE INGREDIENTS → **2 SERVE WITH ICE**

FROZEN FRUITY YOGURT POPS

Who says pops are just for kids? These fruity yogurt pops, packed with vitamin-rich blueberries, are perfect for summery breakfasts on the go, or healthy hot-weather snacks.

MAKES 6–8 • **READY IN** 5 mins, plus freezing
SPECIAL EQUIPMENT Blender or hand-held blender • Ice pop molds

INGREDIENTS

- 2 cups plain yogurt
- 7oz (200g) blueberries
- ⅔ cup confectioner's sugar

1 BLEND THE INGREDIENTS
Place all the ingredients in a blender and blend until smooth, or process them with a hand-held blender.

2 TRANSFER AND FREEZE
Carefully transfer the mixture to the ice pop molds and freeze for at least 2 hours (they will keep in the freezer for up to 8 weeks).

3 RELEASE AND SERVE
To serve, carefully place the molds under hot running water for 1 minute to help release the pops.

Try using other soft fruits, such as strawberries, peaches, or raspberries in place of the blueberries for a range of flavors.

PLAN OF ACTION!

1 BLEND INGREDIENTS → **2 TRANSFER AND FREEZE** → **3 RELEASE AND SERVE**

PERFECT OATMEAL

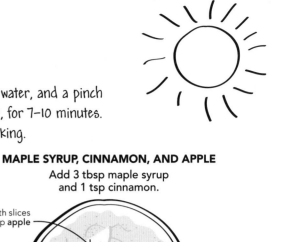

For 1 serving, bring 1 cup rolled oats, ⅔ cup whole milk, ¾ cup water, and a pinch of salt to a boil. Reduce the heat and simmer, stirring constantly, for 7–10 minutes. For these variations, simply add the extra ingredients during cooking.

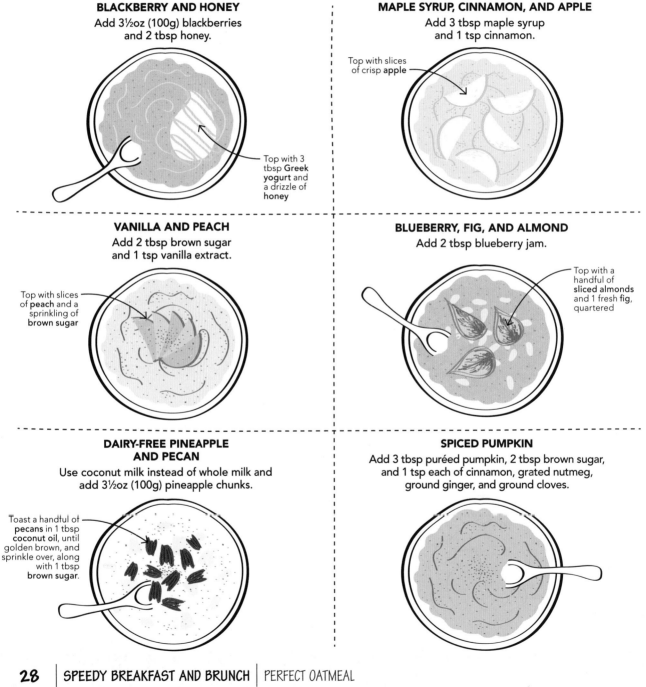

BLACKBERRY AND HONEY
Add 3½oz (100g) blackberries
and 2 tbsp honey.

Top with 3 tbsp **Greek yogurt** and a drizzle of **honey**

MAPLE SYRUP, CINNAMON, AND APPLE
Add 3 tbsp maple syrup
and 1 tsp cinnamon.

Top with slices of crisp **apple**

VANILLA AND PEACH
Add 2 tbsp brown sugar
and 1 tsp vanilla extract.

Top with slices of **peach** and a sprinkling of **brown sugar**

BLUEBERRY, FIG, AND ALMOND
Add 2 tbsp blueberry jam.

Top with a handful of **sliced almonds** and 1 fresh **fig**, quartered

DAIRY-FREE PINEAPPLE AND PECAN
Use coconut milk instead of whole milk and
add 3½oz (100g) pineapple chunks.

Toast a handful of **pecans** in 1 tbsp **coconut oil**, until golden brown, and sprinkle over, along with 1 tbsp **brown sugar**.

SPICED PUMPKIN
Add 3 tbsp puréed pumpkin, 2 tbsp brown sugar,
and 1 tsp each of cinnamon, grated nutmeg,
ground ginger, and ground cloves.

OVERNIGHT OATS

Leave these no-cook oats to soak in a sealed jar in the fridge overnight, then enjoy a delicious instant breakfast the next morning. Simply combine 1 cup rolled oats, 1½ cups liquid, and your choice of flavorings.

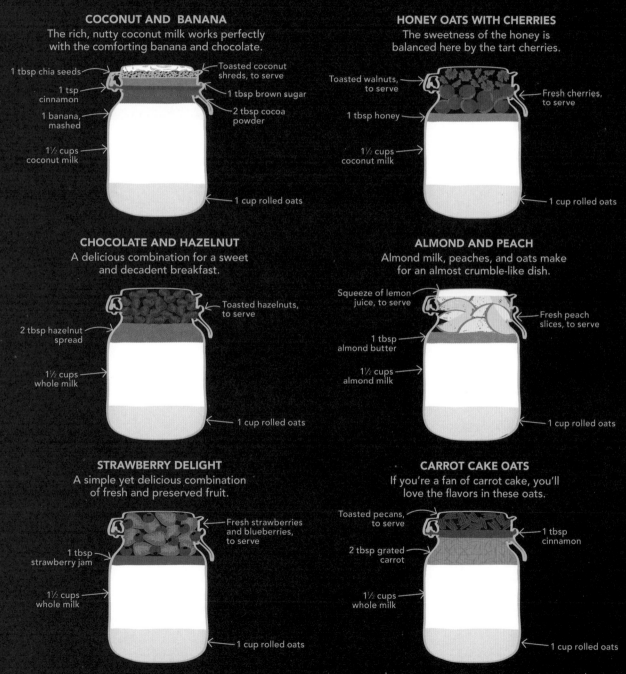

COCONUT AND BANANA
The rich, nutty coconut milk works perfectly with the comforting banana and chocolate.

- 1 tbsp chia seeds
- 1 tsp cinnamon
- 1 banana, mashed
- 1½ cups coconut milk
- Toasted coconut shreds, to serve
- 1 tbsp brown sugar
- 2 tbsp cocoa powder
- 1 cup rolled oats

HONEY OATS WITH CHERRIES
The sweetness of the honey is balanced here by the tart cherries.

- Toasted walnuts, to serve
- 1 tbsp honey
- 1½ cups coconut milk
- Fresh cherries, to serve
- 1 cup rolled oats

CHOCOLATE AND HAZELNUT
A delicious combination for a sweet and decadent breakfast.

- 2 tbsp hazelnut spread
- 1½ cups whole milk
- Toasted hazelnuts, to serve
- 1 cup rolled oats

ALMOND AND PEACH
Almond milk, peaches, and oats make for an almost crumble-like dish.

- Squeeze of lemon juice, to serve
- 1 tbsp almond butter
- 1½ cups almond milk
- Fresh peach slices, to serve
- 1 cup rolled oats

STRAWBERRY DELIGHT
A simple yet delicious combination of fresh and preserved fruit.

- 1 tbsp strawberry jam
- 1½ cups whole milk
- Fresh strawberries and blueberries, to serve
- 1 cup rolled oats

CARROT CAKE OATS
If you're a fan of carrot cake, you'll love the flavors in these oats.

- Toasted pecans, to serve
- 2 tbsp grated carrot
- 1½ cups whole milk
- 1 tbsp cinnamon
- 1 cup rolled oats

INGREDIENTS

1½ cups rolled oats

½ cup mixed seeds, such as sunflower, sesame, pumpkin, and golden flaxseed

⅓ cup mixed unsalted nuts, such as cashews, almonds, hazelnuts, and walnuts

1 tbsp light olive oil, plus extra for greasing

2 tbsp honey

3½ tbsp maple syrup

¼ cup
dried blueberries

¼ cup
dried cranberries

¼ cup
dried cherries

2 tbsp
dried coconut

Greek yogurt or milk,
to serve

QUICK STOVETOP GRANOLA

Making your own granola ensures it's packed with your favorite ingredients, which you can mix and match to your heart's desire. For something a bit more decadent, try drizzling melted chocolate over the granola as it cools.

SERVES 4-6 • **READY IN** 15 mins, plus cooling

❶ TOAST THE OATS, NUTS, AND SEEDS

Place the oats, seeds, and nuts in a large deep-sided frying pan. Heat over medium heat, stirring frequently, for 3–5 minutes or until lightly browned. Transfer to a baking sheet and set aside.

❷ ADD THE OIL, HONEY, AND SYRUP

Heat the oil, honey, and syrup in the frying pan until melted and well combined. Return the toasted oats, nuts, and seeds to the pan and heat for another 5 minutes, stirring frequently, until warmed through and evenly coated.

❸ COMBINE WITH THE DRIED FRUIT

Mix together the berries, cherries, and coconut, add to the pan, and combine well.

❹ LET COOL

Pour the mixture onto the baking sheet, spread it out, and let cool completely. When cold, break the granola into small pieces and transfer to an airtight container. To serve, layer Greek yogurt and granola into four glass dishes. Alternatively, serve with milk.

TIP – This keeps for up to a month in an airtight container. As it gets older, it may benefit from a brief reheating in the oven to crisp up once more.

For lots more granola ideas, see pp32–33.

GRANOLA BLENDS

Do you like your granola sweet and fruity, savory and nutty, or somewhere in between? To create your own perfect blend, use the ingredient and proportion suggestions below, then follow the cooking instructions on pages 30–31. To make muesli instead, simply combine the dry ingredients and enjoy immediately.

DRY INGREDIENTS

Grains, typically rolled oats, form the base of most granolas and muesli. Buckwheat, a grain-like seed, is a great gluten-free option. Nuts and seeds add a wholesome crunch and dried fruit adds sweetness and a softer texture to the blend.

1 GRAINS
Add 3–4 parts of a single grain or a selection of **mixed grains**, such as **rolled oats**, **spelt**, **quinoa**, and **barley**. Try also: rye, buckwheat, or wheatgerm.

2 NUTS
If you like nuts, add 1–2 parts of a single nut or a selection of **mixed nuts**, such as **almonds, pistachios, pecans, hazelnuts**, and **Brazil nuts**. Try also: cashews, macadamias, peanuts, or walnuts.

3 SEEDS
If you enjoy seeds, add 1–2 parts of a single seed or a selection of mixed seeds, such as **pumpkin seeds**, **sesame seeds**, **sunflower seeds**, and **chia seeds**. Try also: hemp seeds, pine nuts, poppy seeds, or flaxseed.

4 DRIED FRUIT
To add sweetness, include 1–2 parts of a single dried fruit or a selection of **mixed dried fruit**, such as **cranberries**, **banana chips**, **mango**, and **dates**. Try also: cherries, apricots, figs, raisins, or golden raisins.

WET INGREDIENTS, SPICES, AND FLAVORINGS

Adding a fat binds the dry ingredients. Spices and flavorings are a delicious optional extra, and a syrup, spread, or preserve helps create sweet, crunchy clusters during cooking.

5 FATS
Add ¼–½ part of **olive oil**, sunflower oil, coconut oil, or melted butter.

6 SPICES AND FLAVORINGS
Why not add a small amount of your favorite spice or flavoring, such as **ground cinnamon** or **vanilla extract**? Try also: grated nutmeg, ground ginger, allspice, almond extract, grated lemon or orange zest, or coconut shavings.

7 SYRUPS, SPREADS, AND PRESERVES
Add ½–1 part of your favorite syrup, spread, or preserve, such as **maple syrup**, **raspberry jam**, or **peanut butter**. Try also: honey, agave nectar, rice syrup, hazelnut spread, fruit jams and preserves, lemon curd, or applesauce.

BANANA AND OAT BRAN MUFFINS

These muffins are a tasty and healthy choice for a late leisurely brunch. There's no need to wait until they cool completely—they're delicious eaten still warm.

MAKES 12   •   **READY IN** 20 mins
SPECIAL EQUIPMENT 12 paper muffin liners and 12-hole muffin pan • electric hand-held mixer

- 8 tbsp butter, softened
- 1 cup all-purpose flour
- 1 tsp baking soda
- 1 tsp baking powder
- 1 tsp ground cinnamon
- ¾ cup oat bran
- ⅓ cup chopped walnuts
- ½ cup brown sugar
- 2 eggs, lightly beaten
- 3 ripe bananas, mashed
- ½ cup whole milk

MIX DRY INGREDIENTS

1 LINE

MUFFIN LINERS

MUFFIN PAN

Preheat oven to 375°F (190°C). Line the muffin pan with muffin liners.

2 SIFT

SIEVE

oat bran

cinnamon

baking powder

baking soda

flour and walnuts

Sift the flour, oat bran, cinnamon, baking soda, and baking powder to aerate them and get rid of lumps. Pour in any oat bran left in the sieve, add the walnuts, and stir well.

MIX WET INGREDIENTS AND COMBINE WITH DRY

3 CREAM

sugar

ELECTRIC MIXER

butter

Cream the butter and sugar together until very light and fluffy.

milk

mashed banana

4 ADD

eggs

Add the beaten eggs and mix well. Then stir in the bananas and milk.

5 POUR

wet mixture

dry mixture

Pour the wet mixture into the dry and stir until just combined (do not over-mix or the muffins will be heavy).

BAKE!

6 DIVIDE

Divide the mixture between the muffin liners, then place the pan in the oven and bake for 15–20 minutes.

7 CHECK

The muffins are ready when a toothpick inserted into one of them comes out clean. Transfer to a wire rack to cool.

To freeze the muffins, wait for them to cool then place them on a baking sheet and put it in the freezer. After about 3 hours, transfer the muffins to a freezer bag and seal.

LEMON AND POPPY SEED MUFFINS

These light and lemony muffins are perfect for a weekend breakfast or brunch—you can eat them immediately and pop the leftovers in an airtight container to have as sweet snacks throughout the week.

MAKES 12 • **READY IN** 20 mins, plus cooling
SPECIAL EQUIPMENT 12-hole muffin pan and 12 paper muffin liners

INGREDIENTS

- 1⅓ cup self-rising flour
- 1 tsp baking powder
- ¼ tsp salt
- ½ cup granulated sugar
- finely grated zest of 1 lemon
- 1 heaping tsp poppy seeds
- ½ cup whole milk
- ½ cup plain yogurt
- 3½ tbsp sunflower oil
- 1 large egg, lightly beaten
- 2 tbsp lemon juice

FOR THE GLAZE
- 2 tbsp lemon juice
- 1¼ cups confectioner's sugar
- finely grated zest of 1 lemon

1 MIX THE DRY INGREDIENTS

Preheat the oven to 400°F (200°C) and line a 12-hole muffin pan with paper muffin liners. Sift the flour, baking powder, and salt into a large bowl. Use a balloon whisk to mix through the sugar, lemon zest, and poppy seeds.

2 MIX WET INGREDIENTS AND COMBINE WITH DRY

Measure the milk, yogurt, and oil into a bowl, then add the egg and lemon juice and beat it all together thoroughly. Pour the liquid into the center of the dry ingredients and mix with a wooden spoon. Stop mixing as soon as the ingredients are combined, as over-mixing can make the muffins tough.

3 DIVIDE AND BAKE

Divide the mixture equally between the muffin liners and bake in the middle of the preheated oven for 15 minutes until the muffins are lightly brown and well risen. Remove from the oven and let them cool in the pan for 5 minutes before transferring to a wire rack to cool completely.

4 DRIZZLE WITH THE GLAZE

For the glaze, mix the lemon juice and confectioner's sugar to a thin icing, drizzle it over the muffins, and sprinkle them with lemon zest.

PLAN OF ACTION! → 1 MIX DRY INGREDIENTS → 2 MIX WET INGREDIENTS → 3 DIVIDE AND BAKE → 4 DRIZZLE WITH GLAZE

QUINOA AND POLENTA MUFFINS

Rich in whole grains, these savory muffins will make a perfect start to your day. Serve them with eggs, bacon, and avocado for a filling and hearty breakfast that's loads tastier than toast!

MAKES 8 • **READY IN** 30 mins
SPECIAL EQUIPMENT 8-hole muffin pan and 8 paper muffin liners

INGREDIENTS

- 1 tbsp light olive oil
- 4 large eggs
- 8 bacon strips
- large pat of butter, to serve
- 2 avocados, pitted and cut into thin slices, to serve

FOR THE BATTER
- ¾ cup polenta
- ⅔ cup whole wheat flour
- 1 cup quinoa, cooked according to package instructions
- 1 tbsp baking powder
- ½ tsp baking soda
- ¾ tsp sea salt
- 1 cup milk
- 3½ tbsp light olive oil
- 1 tbsp honey
- 3 large eggs

1 MIX THE DRY INGREDIENTS

Preheat the oven to 400°F (200°C). Grease and line an 8-hole muffin pan with the paper liners. For the batter, place the polenta, flour, quinoa, baking powder, baking soda, and salt in a large bowl and mix to combine.

2 MIX WET INGREDIENTS AND COMBINE WITH DRY

In a separate bowl, whisk together the milk, oil, honey, and eggs until well combined. Then gently fold the liquid mixture into the dry ingredients and mix until just combined (over-mixing can make the muffins tough).

3 DIVIDE AND BAKE

Divide the batter equally between the 8 muffin liners and transfer the pan to the oven. Bake for about 20 minutes or until a toothpick inserted into the center comes out clean.

4 PREPARE THE EGGS, BACON, AND AVOCADO

Meanwhile, heat the oil in a frying pan over medium heat and cook the eggs. Then add the bacon strips and cook until crisp. Split the muffins, top with some butter, and serve with the fried eggs, bacon, and avocado.

PLAN OF ACTION!
1 MIX DRY INGREDIENTS → 2 COMBINE WET AND DRY INGREDIENTS → 3 DIVIDE AND BAKE → 4 PREP EGGS, BACON, AND AVOCADO

TOAST TOPPINGS

Smoky aïoli, fried egg, and crispy bacon bits on toasted crusty bread

Soft cheese, such as **Brie** or soft goat cheese

Very ripe fresh **figs**

Soft cheese, figs, and prosciutto on a toasted bagel

For the **aïoli**, process 3 tbsp mayo, 2 cloves of garlic (crushed), and ½ tsp chipotle or smoked paprika in a food processor.

Wilt the **spinach** in a frying pan over medium heat before draining off excess liquid.

Soft goat cheese, pear slices, and honey on white toast

Wilted spinach, scrambled eggs, and feta cheese on toasted rye

Toast doesn't have to be on the side—it can take center stage too! With a little imagination and a handful of ingredients you can transform the humble slice into a stand-alone sensation. Experiment with different breads as well as toppings for the ultimate open sandwich. Here are a few ideas to tempt your toast-loving taste buds!

Cream cheese, smoked salmon, red onions, tomatoes, and capers on toasted pumpernickel

Peanut butter, banana, crushed walnuts, cinnamon, and honey on white toast

Plain yogurt, peach slices, and honey on white toast

Drizzle of **olive oil**

Sea salt and freshly ground **black pepper**

Mashed avocado and slices of hard-boiled egg on multigrain toast

INGREDIENTS

¼ cup cream cheese

4 slices of challah bread or brioche, each 1in (2.5cm) thick

4–6 strawberries, hulled and thickly sliced

2 eggs

⅓ cup light brown sugar

¼ cup milk

½ tsp vanilla extract

½ tsp ground cinnamon

2 tbsp butter

honey, to serve

STRAWBERRY-STUFFED FRENCH TOAST

This is a decadent and delicious take on the brunch classic, French toast. Here, the bread is sandwiched together with softened cream cheese and juicy strawberries to make a deluxe version that's even tastier than the original!

MAKES 2 • **READY IN** 20 mins

1 ASSEMBLE THE SLICES

Spread 1 tablespoon of the cream cheese over each slice of bread. Top 2 bread slices with 2–3 strawberries each, then cover with the remaining bread slices to make 2 sandwiches.

2 DIP IN THE EGG MIXTURE

In a bowl, whisk together the eggs, sugar, milk, vanilla extract, and cinnamon with a balloon whisk. Dip the sandwiches in the egg mixture, submerging them completely.

3 PAN FRY THE SANDWICHES

In a frying pan, melt 1 tablespoon of butter over medium heat. Pan fry the sandwiches for 3–4 minutes on each side, or until golden brown. Add the remaining butter to the pan, as needed. Serve hot, drizzled with honey.

BUTTERMILK PANCAKES

Making pancakes with buttermilk rather than whole milk makes for a deliciously light and airy texture. These are perfect fare for a lazy morning.

MAKES 20 • **READY IN** 10–12 mins

- 2 tbsp butter, melted and cooled, plus extra for cooking and serving
- ⅔ cup buttermilk
- ½ cup whole milk
- 2 large eggs, lightly beaten
- 1 tsp vanilla extract
- 1½ cups self-rising flour, sifted
- 1 tsp baking powder
- 2 tbsp granulated sugar
- maple syrup, to serve

PREPARE THE WET INGREDIENTS

1 MELT

SMALL SAUCEPAN

butter

Melt the butter over low heat.

You can use all whole milk in this recipe, rather than whole milk and buttermilk, if you prefer.

2 MIX

Add cooled melted butter.

milk

buttermilk

vanilla extract

2 eggs

JUG

Measure the buttermilk and whole milk into a jug, then add the other wet ingredients. Whisk everything together with a fork.

MAKE THE BATTER

3 COMBINE

granulated sugar

baking powder

WOODEN SPOON

Flour

Combine the dry ingredients.

4 MIX TOGETHER

wet mixture

WHISK

Pour the wet mixture into a well in the center of the flour mixture and whisk together.

COOK IN BATCHES

5 COOK

LADLE

batter

melt the butter

Pour out the mixture to form 3¼–4in (8–10cm) pancakes.

6 FLIP AND SERVE

Flip when small bubbles appear.

SPATULA

Cook the pancakes for about 2 minutes on each side.

PANCAKE TOPPINGS

For chocolate pancakes, add 3 tbsp **cocoa powder** and ¼ cup **chocolate chips** to the batter.

Mascarpone, peaches, and honey with fresh mint leaves

Chocolate pancakes with hazelnut spread and crushed raspberries

Very ripe fresh **peaches**

For the **caramelized banana**, melt 2 tbsp each of **butter** and **brown sugar**, add slices of **banana**, and cook until golden brown.

Caramelized banana and crushed walnuts

Blueberry pancakes with crispy bacon slices and maple syrup

Blueberries and maple syrup are a firm favorite, but why not pile your pancakes with something a little different? Whether you want to satisfy your sweet tooth or have a soft spot for something savory, here are some tasty and tempting topping ideas. See pages 42–3 for the basic pancake recipe.

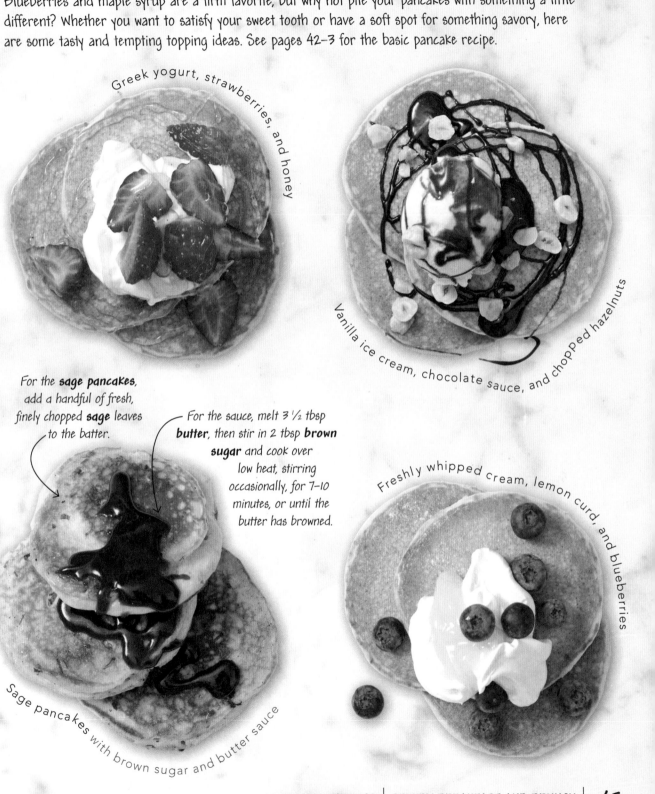

Greek yogurt, strawberries, and honey

Vanilla ice cream, chocolate sauce, and chopped hazelnuts

For the **sage pancakes**, add a handful of fresh, finely chopped **sage** leaves to the batter.

For the sauce, melt 3 ½ tbsp **butter**, then stir in 2 tbsp **brown sugar** and cook over low heat, stirring occasionally, for 7–10 minutes, or until the butter has browned.

Freshly whipped cream, lemon curd, and blueberries

Sage pancakes with brown sugar and butter sauce

PANCAKE TOPPINGS | **SPEEDY BREAKFAST AND BRUNCH** | **45**

INGREDIENTS

2 cups self-rising flour, sifted

1 tsp baking powder

2 tbsp superfine sugar

⅔ cup buttermilk

½ cup whole milk

2 large eggs

1 tsp vanilla extract

2 tbsp butter, melted and cooled, plus extra for cooking, and to serve

5½oz (150g) blueberries

maple syrup, to serve

BLUEBERRY PANCAKES

This is the classic pancake combination. It's made here with tangy buttermilk for a lighter batter, but substitute whole milk if you prefer. If you've got friends over, why not take turns cooking and eating for a relaxed weekend brunch?

MAKES 20 • **READY IN** 20 mins

1 MIX THE DRY INGREDIENTS

Use a large balloon whisk to mix together the flour, baking powder, and sugar in a large bowl.

2 WHISK THE WET INGREDIENTS

Measure the buttermilk and milk into a large liquid measuring cup, then add the eggs and vanilla extract and whisk it well. Whisk in the cooled, melted butter.

3 MAKE THE BATTER

Make a well in the center of the flour and slowly whisk in the milk mixture, using the whisk to bring in the flour gradually from the edges of the well, until it has formed a thick batter.

4 ADD THE BLUEBERRIES

Heat a pat of butter in a frying pan and pour out 4in (10cm) pancakes. Once you have poured them into the pan, sprinkle some of the blueberries on top; the batter will rise up around the berries as they cook.

5 COOK AND FLIP

Cook the pancakes for 2 minutes on each side, turning when the edges are set and bubbles appear and pop on the surface. When cooked, keep them warm on a plate under a clean kitchen towel while you cook the rest. Serve with butter and maple syrup, or see pp44–45 for more topping ideas.

TIP – Frozen blueberries are good value and work just as well as fresh fruit, so you can save money and cook these out of season, too. Add the berries straight from the freezer; they will defrost and cook at the same time as the pancakes and won't break down too much either.

Try adding
1 heaping tsp ground cinnamon to the batter for a spicy-sweet, aromatic flavor.

PUMPKIN AND CINNAMON WAFFLES

Adding spices and canned pumpkin to these waffles gives them a lovely autumnal flavor. If you can't find canned pumpkin purée, make your own by roasting and puréeing a fresh pumpkin.

SERVES 6 • **READY IN** 20 mins

SPECIAL EQUIPMENT Waffle maker or waffle iron

INGREDIENTS

- 1¼ cups self-rising flour, sifted
- ⅓ cup light brown sugar
- 1 tsp baking powder
- 2 tsp ground cinnamon
- 2 large eggs, separated
- 1¼ cups whole milk
- 1 tsp vanilla extract
- 4 tbsp butter, melted and cooled
- 5½oz (150g) canned pumpkin purée
- maple syrup, sliced bananas, or fried apple wedges, to serve

1 MIX TOGETHER THE DRY AND WET INGREDIENTS

In a bowl, use a balloon whisk to mix the flour, brown sugar, baking powder, and cinnamon. Whisk in the egg yolks, milk, vanilla extract, melted butter, and pumpkin purée.

2 WHISK THE EGG WHITES

Preheat the waffle maker or iron. Using a clean whisk, whisk the egg whites to firm peaks. Stir the pumpkin mixture into the flour mixture until evenly combined.

3 BAKE THE WAFFLES

Preheat the oven to 250°F (130°C). Pour a small ladleful of the batter onto the waffle maker or iron and spread almost to the edge. Close the lid and bake until golden. Keep warm in a single layer in the oven while you make the rest of the waffles.

4 SERVE IMMEDIATELY

Serve immediately with maple syrup, sliced bananas, or buttery fried apple wedges.

PLAN OF ACTION!

1 MIX DRY AND WET INGREDIENTS → **2** WHISK EGG WHITES → **3** BAKE WAFFLES → **4** SERVE IMMEDIATELY

CORNMEAL WAFFLES WITH BACON MAPLE SAUCE

These easy-to-make cornmeal waffles are a delicious twist on the brunch classic. The cornmeal adds a slight crunch and a delicate, moist sweetness to the waffles—a perfect base for the sweet-and-savory sauce.

MAKES 6-8 • **READY IN** 20 mins

SPECIAL EQUIPMENT Waffle maker or waffle iron

INGREDIENTS

- ¾ cup all-purpose flour
- ½ cup cornmeal or fine polenta
- 1 tsp baking powder
- 2 tbsp granulated sugar
- 1¼ cups milk
- 5 tbsp unsalted butter, melted
- 1 tsp vanilla extract
- 2 large eggs, separated
- 4 strips smoked bacon
- ½ cup good-quality maple syrup
- jam, fresh fruit, sweetened cream, or ice cream, to serve (optional)

❶ MIX TOGETHER THE DRY AND WET INGREDIENTS

Place the flour, cornmeal or polenta, baking powder, and sugar in a bowl. Make a well in the center and pour in the milk, butter, vanilla extract, and egg yolks. Using a balloon whisk, gradually whisk together the ingredients.

❷ WHISK THE EGG WHITES

Preheat the waffle maker or iron. In a clean, large bowl, whisk the egg whites until soft peaks form. Fold into the batter with a metal spoon.

❸ BAKE THE WAFFLES

Preheat the oven to 250°F (130°C). Pour a small ladleful of the batter onto the waffle maker or iron and spread almost to the edge. Close the lid and bake until golden. Keep warm in a single layer in the oven while you make the rest of the waffles.

❹ MAKE THE BACON MAPLE SAUCE AND SERVE

While the waffles are baking, make the sauce. In a frying pan, dry-fry the bacon until crispy. When cool enough to handle, crumble the bacon. Gently heat the maple syrup in a small, heavy-bottomed saucepan over low heat. Add the bacon to the warm syrup before pouring over the waffles. Serve immediately with jam, fresh fruit, sweetened cream, or ice cream, if desired.

PLAN OF ACTION! ❶ MIX DRY AND WET INGREDIENTS → ❷ WHISK EGG WHITES → ❸ BAKE WAFFLES → ❹ MAKE SAUCE AND SERVE

EGGS 6 WAYS

1 SOFT-BOILED

1 Half-fill a pan with water and bring to a boil. Add a pinch of salt (this keeps the white from "leaking" if the shell cracks).

2 Using a slotted spoon, carefully lower the egg into the water.

3 Boil for 4–6 minutes (depending on the size of the egg, and how runny you like the yolk).

4 Remove the egg from the pan and serve immediately.

2 POACHED

1 Bring a large pan of water to a boil. Add a pinch of salt and a splash of white wine vinegar (to help bind the egg white).

2 Crack a very fresh egg into a small bowl.

3 Vigorously stir the water in the pan to create a vortex, then carefully pour the egg into the center.

4 Reduce the heat and cook for 2–4 minutes (depending on the size of the egg and how you like the yolk). Serve hot.

3 FRIED

"SUNNY SIDE UP"

1 Melt a pat of butter or a splash of olive oil in a frying pan over medium heat.

2 Crack an egg into the pan and fry for 5–6 minutes, or until the white has firmed. Season and serve hot.

"OVER EASY"

1 For an egg fried on both sides, crack an egg into a heated greased pan (see step 1, above) and fry for 2–3 minutes.

2 Add salt to taste, then flip the egg, using a spatula, and fry for an additional 2 minutes. Serve hot.

Eggs are versatile, quick-cooking, and nutritious—ideal for a speedy breakfast or brunch. As well as trying these classic methods, why not add grated cheese, pieces of cooked ham, or sliced scallions to your scrambled eggs—or pop some wilted spinach into the ramekins before cooking baked eggs?

④ EGG IN A HOLE

1 Use a 3in (7.5cm) round cookie cutter to cut a hole in the center of a piece of toast.

2 Melt a pat of butter in a frying pan over medium heat and add the toast.

3 Crack an egg into the hole and cook for 2–3 minutes. Add salt, to taste.

4 Flip the toast and egg, using a spatula, and cook for an additional 2–3 minutes. Serve hot.

⑤ SCRAMBLED

1 Crack 2–3 eggs into a large bowl. Add 2 tbsp water or milk, and salt and pepper to taste.

2 Melt a pat of butter in a frying pan over medium heat.

3 Pour in the eggs and cook, stirring frequently with a wooden spoon, for 8–10 minutes, or until set.

4 Serve hot, with toast.

⑥ BAKED

1 Preheat the oven to 350°F (180°C) and bring 2 eggs to room temperature.

2 Lightly grease 2 ramekins or egg cups. Crack an egg into each, and season with salt and pepper to taste.

3 Bake on the center rack of the oven for 17–20 minutes, or until set.

4 Remove from the oven and serve hot with buttered toast.

EGGS BENEDICT WITH BACON AND WALNUT BREAD

Crisp, salty bacon and crunchy walnut bread lift this breakfast classic to a whole new level. It's best enjoyed immediately, while the yolk and sauce are still hot and runny.

SERVES 2 • **READY IN** 15 mins
SPECIAL EQUIPMENT Blender or food processor

INGREDIENTS

FOR THE HOLLANDAISE SAUCE
- 7 tbsp unsalted butter
- 1 large egg yolk
- ½ tbsp lemon juice
- salt and freshly ground black pepper

FOR THE REST
- 6 strips of smoked bacon
- 4 eggs
- 4 thick slices of walnut bread, or multigrain bread, crusts removed

① MAKE THE HOLLANDAISE

Melt the butter over low heat. Put the egg yolk, lemon juice, and seasoning into a blender and process briefly. With the motor running, pour in the melted butter drop by drop, accelerating to a thin stream, until the butter is fully combined with the other ingredients to create a thick sauce. Serve as soon as possible.

② BROIL THE BACON

Meanwhile, preheat the broiler to its highest setting. Cut each bacon strip in half horizontally, to make 12 short pieces, and broil until crisp. Keep warm.

③ POACH THE EGGS

Boil a large pan of salted water, then reduce the heat to a low simmer. Crack an egg into a small cup and gently slide into the bubbling water. Repeat for all the eggs. Poach for 3 minutes, until the white is set but the yolk is still runny. Remove with a slotted spoon.

④ TOAST THE BREAD

Meanwhile, toast the bread. When toasted, top each piece with 3 half pieces of crispy bacon, a poached egg, and a little hollandaise sauce.

TIP – Use the freshest eggs you can find, as these will hold together better when you're poaching them. At step 3, use a spoon to stir the water so that a whirlpool forms, and pour the eggs into the center. This helps keep the egg white together, as does adding a teaspoonful of vinegar to the boiling water.

If you want to try the original dish, eggs Benedict is traditionally made with ham and a toasted English muffin instead of bacon and walnut bread. Smoked salmon is also delicious in place of ham.

PLAN OF ACTION!

① **MAKE HOLLANDAISE** → ② **BROIL BACON** → ③ **POACH EGGS** → ④ **TOAST BREAD**

CROQUE-MADAME

This easy version of the French café staple uses three layers of melting Gruyère cheese in place of the traditional creamy sauce. It's the ultimate toasted ham and cheese!

MAKES 4 • **READY IN** 20 mins

INGREDIENTS

- 2 tbsp butter, plus extra for the bread
- 8 slices of good-quality white bread
- 7oz (200g) grated Gruyère cheese
- 1 tbsp Dijon mustard (optional)
- salt and freshly ground black pepper
- 4 thick slices of good-quality ham, or 5½oz (150g) thinly sliced ham
- 1 tbsp sunflower oil
- 4 small eggs

❶ ASSEMBLE THE SANDWICHES

Butter each slice of bread on both sides. Set aside 1¾oz (50g) of the grated cheese to top the sandwiches in step 3. Now make the sandwiches by spreading 4 slices of bread with a little mustard (if using), then a layer of grated cheese, firmly pressed down. Season with salt and pepper to taste, then add a slice of ham, another layer of cheese, and a second slice of bread.

❷ BROWN THEM OFF

Melt the 2 tablespoons of butter in a large, non-stick frying pan and cook 2 sandwiches carefully over medium heat for 2–3 minutes on each side, pressing them gently with a spatula, until golden brown. Keep warm while you cook the remaining 2 sandwiches. Wipe the pan with paper towels.

❸ MELT THE CHEESE

Preheat the broiler to its highest setting. Place the fried sandwiches on a baking sheet and top each with one quarter of the reserved grated cheese. Broil until the cheese has melted and is bubbling.

❹ FRY THE EGGS

Meanwhile, heat the sunflower oil in the frying pan and fry the eggs to your liking. Top each sandwich with a fried egg and eat immediately.

PLAN OF ACTION! ❶ ASSEMBLE SANDWICHES → ❷ BROWN THEM OFF → ❸ MELT CHEESE → ❹ FRY EGGS

CLASSIC OMELET

The ultimate fast food, omelets are extremely quick to make and very tasty too—perfect for a nutritious and satisfying breakfast or brunch.

MAKES 1 • **READY IN** 5 mins

- 3 eggs
- salt and freshly ground black pepper
- pat of butter

10 MINS OR LESS!

BEAT AND SEASON EGGS

WHISK

1 BEAT

salt

pepper

eggs

2 MELT

egg and butter mixture

NONSTICK FRYING PAN

Melt a pat of butter over medium heat and add the egg mixture.

COOK EGGS

3 TILT

Tilt the pan to spread the egg mixture evenly. Stir the eggs with a fork, stopping as soon as they're set.

FORK

A 3-egg omelet is easiest to fold—any more than 6 will be more difficult.

FOLD AND SERVE

4 FOLD

half-folded omelet

Fold the side of the omelet nearest the handle halfway over itself.

5 TAP

neatly rolled omelet

Sharply tap the handle so the bottom side of the omelet curls over. Slide the omelet to the edge of the pan.

6 SERVE

PLATE

Tilt the pan over a plate so the omelet rolls "seam side" down.

CHEESE SOUFFLÉ OMELET

PLAN OF ACTION!

Why not jazz up an easy omelet by making it soufflé-style, with airy egg whites and oozy cheese? The lovely texture of the omelet is rapidly lost as it cools, so eat it immediately, with a green salad or crusty bread on the side, if you like.

MAKES 1 • **READY IN** 20 mins

❶ MAKE THE SAUCE

Heat the butter in a saucepan. Add the corn and red bell pepper, stir, then cover and cook very gently for 5 minutes or until tender. Stir in the cornstarch, followed by the milk. Bring to a boil and cook for 2 minutes, stirring all the time, until thick. Stir in the chives, cheeses, cayenne, salt, and pepper to taste.

❷ PREPARE THE EGGS

Beat the egg yolks with 2 tablespoons of water and add salt and pepper. Whisk the egg whites until stiff and fold into the yolks with a metal spoon.

❸ COOK THE OMELET

Preheat the broiler. Heat a pat of butter in a non-stick frying pan, add the egg mixture, and gently spread it out. Cook over medium heat for about 3 minutes until golden underneath. Immediately place the pan under the broiler and cook for 2–3 minutes until risen and golden on top. Meanwhile, reheat the sauce, stirring.

❹ FLIP, FOLD, AND GARNISH

Slide the omelet out onto a plate. Quickly spread one half with the cheese and corn sauce (don't worry if it oozes over the edge). Flip the uncovered side over the top to fold the omelet in half, and garnish with a few snipped chives. Serve immediately.

INGREDIENTS

2 eggs, separated

pat of butter

FOR THE SAUCE

pat of butter

handful of fresh or thawed frozen corn kernels

½ small red bell pepper, seeded and finely chopped

2 tsp cornstarch

7 tbsp milk

2 tsp snipped chives, plus a few extra to garnish

¾oz (20g) Gruyère cheese, grated

¾oz (20g) Cheddar cheese, grated

pinch of cayenne pepper

salt and freshly ground black pepper

BREAKFAST BURRITOS

A great all-in-one breakfast, these Mexican-inspired burritos are perfect for a weekend brunch. If you've got leftovers, pop them in the fridge and microwave for an easy on-the-go weekday breakfast.

MAKES 4 • **READY IN** 20 mins

❶ PREPARE THE FILLINGS

Preheat the broiler to its highest setting and broil the bacon until it is crispy. Meanwhile, heat half the oil in a large, non-stick frying pan, add the potatoes, and cook until crispy all over, then set aside. Wipe the pan with paper towels. Mix the ketchup with the smoked paprika or harissa paste.

❷ SCRAMBLE THE EGGS

Once the bacon and potatoes are ready, make the scrambled eggs. Whisk the eggs with the cream and season well. Heat the butter in the frying pan and cook the egg mixture over low heat until they are barely cooked and still quite loose.

❸ ASSEMBLE THE TORTILLAS

At the same time, lay out the tortillas and put 3 slices of bacon in a line across the middle of each. Top each with one-quarter of the potatoes, still keeping in a line across the center, and add a smear of the spicy ketchup. Finish each by topping with one-quarter of the scrambled eggs and one-quarter of the cheese, again remembering to keep the filling in a compact rectangle down the middle of each tortilla.

❹ ROLL THE BURRITOS

To make the burritos, tuck the sides in over the filling, then roll the longer top and bottom edges up and over the filling, to make a parcel. Press down gently.

❺ BROWN THEM OFF

Heat the remaining 1 tablespoon of oil in a clean frying pan. Put the burritos seam-side down into the pan and cook for 2–3 minutes over medium heat, until golden brown and crispy. Press down with a spatula to seal. Turn carefully and cook for another 2–3 minutes. Depending on the size of your pan you may need to do this in 2 batches. Serve the burritos sliced in half diagonally, with extra spicy ketchup (if desired).

Fried sausage pieces, mushrooms, tomatoes, or even chiles are all great alternative fillings.

PREPARE FILLINGS → **SCRAMBLE EGGS** → **ASSEMBLE TORTILLAS** → **ROLL BURRITOS** → **BROWN THEM**

INGREDIENTS

12 smoked strips of thick-cut bacon

2 tbsp sunflower oil

9oz (250g) cooked, cold potatoes, cut into ½in (1cm) cubes

4 eggs

6 tbsp ketchup, plus extra to serve (optional)

1 tsp smoked paprika or harissa paste

1 tbsp heavy cream

salt and freshly ground black pepper

1 tbsp butter

4 x 8in (20cm) tortilla wraps

3½oz (100g) grated cheese, such as Cheddar

SHAKSHOUKA

This spicy, one-pot breakfast is popular across the Middle East. Serve it with crusty bread or flatbreads to mop up the egg yolks and the deliciously savory sauce.

SERVES 4 • **READY IN** 20 mins

- 2 tbsp olive oil
- 1 onion, halved and finely chopped
- 2 red or green bell peppers, finely chopped
- 2 garlic cloves, finely chopped
- 1 red chile, seeded and finely chopped
- 1 tsp sugar
- 1 x 14oz (400g) can chopped tomatoes
- salt and freshly ground black pepper
- 4 large eggs
- small bunch of flat-leaf parsley, finely chopped

COOK THE VEGGIES

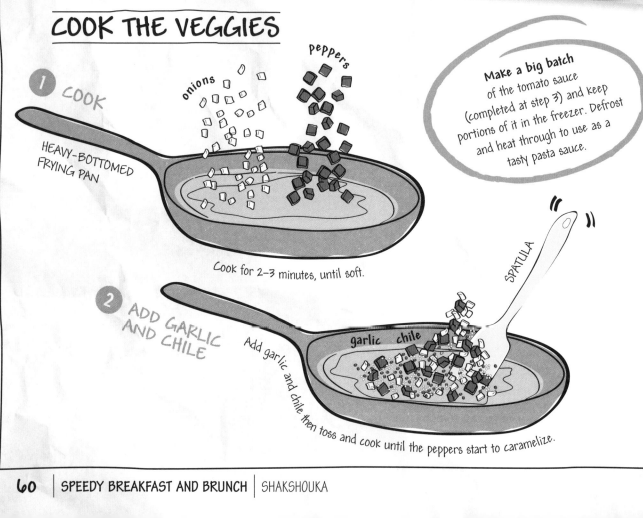

1 COOK

onions

peppers

HEAVY-BOTTOMED FRYING PAN

Cook for 2–3 minutes, until soft.

Make a big batch of the tomato sauce (completed at step 3) and keep portions of it in the freezer. Defrost and heat through to use as a tasty pasta sauce.

2 ADD GARLIC AND CHILE

SPATULA

garlic   chile

Add garlic and chile then toss and cook until the peppers start to caramelize.

tomatoes sugar

salt

pepper

COOK THE TOMATOES AND SUGAR OVER MEDIUM HEAT FOR 3-4 MINS, THEN SEASON WELL WITH SALT AND PEPPER..

3 ADD TOMATOES

COOK THE EGGS

4 CRACK EGGS IN

eggs

Make indentations with a spoon.

Crack eggs into the indentations in the sauce.

COVER AND COOK

5

Cook until the egg whites are set and the yolks are done to your liking.

parsley

6 GARNISH AND SERVE

Remove the lid and scatter with chopped parsley.

POTATO, PANCETTA, AND RED ONION HASH

A hash is perfect if you crave something a little more substantial in the morning. Try serving each portion topped with a fried egg—keep the yolks runny, if you like them that way, as they will form a "sauce" for the hash.

SERVES 2 • **READY IN** 20 mins

1 BOIL THE POTATOES

Bring a pan of salted water to a boil, add the potatoes, and cook for 10 minutes. Drain.

2 COOK THE ONION, BELL PEPPER, AND PANCETTA

Meanwhile, heat the oil in a large, non-stick frying pan over medium heat and cook the onions and red bell pepper for 5 minutes. Add the pancetta, season well, and cook for another 5 minutes, stirring occasionally.

3 BROWN THE POTATOES

Add the boiled potatoes to the frying pan and cook over high heat for about 10 minutes, stirring frequently.

4 GARNISH AND SERVE

Divide the hash between warmed plates and sprinkle with the chives. Serve with a grating of Cheddar cheese or, if you prefer, baked beans and ketchup.

TIP – This meal is a great way to use up leftover cooked potatoes—just cut them into bite-sized chunks and skip straight to step 2.

To add warmth to the dish, add 1 tsp of chile powder or hot smoked paprika (pimentón picante) at step 2.

1	2	3	4
BOIL POTATOES	**COOK VEGGIES AND PANCETTA**	**BROWN POTATOES**	**GARNISH AND SERVE**

INGREDIENTS

salt and freshly ground black pepper

1lb 2oz (500g) floury potatoes, such as Russet, peeled and cut into bite-sized chunks

2 tsp olive oil

1 red onion, finely chopped

½ red bell pepper, diced

1¾oz (50g) chopped pancetta

1 tbsp finely chopped chives

1¾oz (50g) grated mature Cheddar cheese, to serve

LUNCH IN A FLASH
OR ON THE GO

INGREDIENTS

4 large, crusty white
bread rolls

6 ripe, medium
tomatoes, sliced

½ small red bell pepper,
cut into thin strips

3 scallions, white parts
only, sliced

4 hard-boiled eggs,
peeled and
sliced crosswise

leaves from 1 small celery
head, chopped

16 small black olives,
pitted, kept whole
or halved

FOR THE VINAIGRETTE

6 anchovy fillets, packed in
oil or salt

¾ cup olive oil

2½ tbsp red or white
wine vinegar

salt and freshly ground
black pepper

PLAN OF ACTION!

1 MAKE VINAIGRETTE → **2** ASSEMBLE SANDWICHES → **3** FINISH OFF AND SERVE

10 MINS OR LESS!

PAN BAGNA

This sandwich is sure to pep up your lunchbox repertoire! The vinaigrette dresses the fillings and moistens the bread, which explains its name—*pan bagna* means "bathed bread" in the local Provençal dialect.

SERVES 4 • **READY IN** 10 mins

- -

1 MAKE THE VINAIGRETTE

For the vinaigrette, drain and rinse the anchovy fillets, pat dry on paper towels, and chop finely. Place in a bowl and add the oil and vinegar. Stir well and season.

2 ASSEMBLE THE SANDWICHES

On a work surface, slice the bread rolls horizontally in half and place cut-sides up. Place a spoonful of vinaigrette on the bottom half of each roll and spread well. Add the tomatoes, red bell pepper, scallions, eggs, celery leaves, and olives. Season lightly.

3 FINISH OFF AND SERVE

Spread the remaining vinaigrette over the top. Add the top half of each roll. Set on plates and press down each sandwich gently but firmly. Leave for 2–3 minutes, then cut in half and serve.

TIP – If you're making this for a lunchbox, pack the vinaigrette separately in a well-sealed container and add to the sandwich just before eating. This will ensure that you don't have a soggy sandwich when it's lunchtime!

SANDWICH SELECTOR

Mix fresh or canned **white crabmeat** with **lemon juice**, **black pepper**, sliced **apple**, and **micro greens**. For added kick, mix through some **harissa paste**.

For the horseradish mayo, mix 1½ tbsp **mayo** with ½ tbsp **horseradish**.

Roast beef on rye

Layer slices of cooked **roast beef**, **sweet red bell peppers**, **watercress**, and **horseradish mayo**.

Crab and apple on a toasted bagel

For the honey chicken, brown ½ **chicken breast**, chopped, in a little **olive oil** over medium heat. Stir in 1 tbsp **honey** and cook until caramelized.

Mix cooked, **shredded chicken** with **barbecue sauce**, and layer with sliced **avocado** and **arugula leaves**.

Combine the **honey chicken** with thinly sliced **red onion**, fresh **cilantro**, and **sesame seeds**.

For the barbecue sauce, combine 2 tbsp **ketchup**, ½ tbsp each of **brown sugar**, **cider vinegar**, and **Worcestershire sauce**, and a pinch each of **sweet paprika**, **cayenne pepper**, and **garlic powder**.

Barbecue chicken on white

Honey chicken on a sesame seed roll

- - - - Transform the tired lunchtime staple into a truly gourmet experience with a little imagination and a few well-spent minutes. Light and fresh, rich and smoky, or crisp and crunchy—there's the perfect filling for every taste! Experiment with different breads, too.

Polish sausage on a baguette

Combine slices of **Polish sausage** with **sautéed onions** and **bell peppers**, and **whole-grain mustard**.

For the **onions** and **peppers**, sauté ½ **onion** and ½ **pepper** in a drizzle of **olive oil** with **salt** and **pepper** until soft.

Club sandwich on foccacia

Add layers of **chipotle aïoli** (see p38), **Cheddar cheese with chile**, cooked **turkey**, **roasted red bell peppers**, crispy **bacon**, and fresh **spinach**.

Hummus and red bell pepper on multiseed

Layer **hummus**, sliced **cucumbers**, **red bell peppers**, and **alfalfa sprouts** (or **cress**, if you prefer).

Turkey and pesto on sourdough

Layer **pesto** (see p136), **havarti cheese** (substitute **Emmental** or **Edam**, if you prefer), cooked **turkey**, **fresh spinach**, and a dollop of **mayo**.

BEET, GOAT CHEESE, AND ARUGULA SANDWICHES

10 MINS OR LESS!

These are perfect for a picnic or packed lunch, or try them at home with toasted bread instead. Sweet, earthy beets are delicious with the more substantial texture of sourdough or rustic bread.

SERVES 4 • **READY IN** 10 mins

INGREDIENTS

- 8 large slices sourdough or other rustic bread
- butter, softened, for spreading
- 7oz (200g) soft goat cheese
- freshly ground black pepper
- 4 small beets, pre-cooked and sliced
- 2 handfuls of arugula leaves

❶ PREPARE THE BREAD

Spread the slices of bread with butter on one side only. Spread 4 slices with one-quarter each of the goat cheese, season with a little pepper, then add a layer of the beet slices.

❷ ASSEMBLE AND SERVE

Top the beets with a layer of the arugula and finish the sandwich with a final slice of bread, buttered-side down. Cut in half to serve, or pack into a container for transportation.

TIP – These sandwiches use pre-cooked beets to cut down on time (pickled or vacuum-packed both work well), but you can roast your own, if you prefer. Preheat the oven to 400°F (200°C). Cut 4 small beets (approximately 2¼in (75g) each), into ¼in (5mm) slices. Place the slices on a baking sheet, brush them with olive oil, and season well. Bake at the top of the oven for 20 minutes, turning once, until they are lightly browned and cooked through. Remove them from the oven and let cool before starting on step 1.

Why not try using roast or sun-dried tomatoes in place of the beets?

PLAN OF ACTION! ❶ PREP THE BREAD ⟶ ❷ ASSEMBLE AND SERVE

BACON, LETTUCE, AND TOMATO SANDWICH

Zesty lemon and basil mayo lifts this BLT sandwich to another level. The classic sandwich combination remains a lunchtime favorite, and is perfect for the weekend—rather than a lunchbox—as the bacon is best served warm.

SERVES 1 • **READY IN** 15 mins

INGREDIENTS

FOR THE LEMON AND BASIL MAYO
- 2 tbsp good-quality mayonnaise
- 2 tsp lemon juice
- 1 tbsp finely chopped basil leaves
- salt and freshly ground black pepper

FOR THE REST
- 3 slices of applewood or other good-quality bacon
- 2 thickly cut slices of good-quality bread
- 2 tbsp unsalted butter, softened
- 2 large Romaine lettuce leaves, stalks removed and roughly chopped
- 1 medium tomato, sliced

1 MAKE THE MAYO

Preheat the broiler to its highest setting. To make the lemon and basil mayo, mix together the mayonnaise, lemon juice, and basil. Season with salt and pepper to taste and set aside.

2 BROIL THE BACON

Preheat a grill pan or a large, cast-iron frying pan. While it is heating, broil the bacon under the broiler for 2–3 minutes on each side until crispy. Drain on paper towels and keep warm.

3 PREPARE AND TOAST THE BREAD

Spread a little butter on both sides of the bread slices and broil them for 2 minutes on each side, until nicely toasted. Alternatively, omit the butter and simply toast the bread in a toaster.

4 ASSEMBLE AND SERVE

Remove the bread slices from the heat. Spread one side of the toast with a little of the mayonnaise, then top it with the lettuce, tomatoes, and bacon. Finish with a final layer of mayonnaise and top with the second slice of bread. Cut in half to serve.

PLAN OF ACTION! ➊ **MAKE MAYO** ⟶ ➋ **BROIL BACON** ⟶ ➌ **PREP AND TOAST BREAD** ⟶ ➍ **ASSEMBLE AND SERVE**

INGREDIENTS

1 Cuban or French
bread loaf

yellow mustard

4 slices of leftover
roast pork

4 slices of ham

4 slices of Swiss cheese

4 pickled gherkins,
sliced lengthwise

butter, softened

PLAN OF ACTION!

① PREPARE SANDWICHES → ② TOAST AND SERVE

CUBANO

A Latin American variation of a toasted ham and cheese sandwich, pepped up with gherkins and mustard, the Cubano is one of the most popular street foods in Miami. Bring the streets to your kitchen with this make-at-home version!

SERVES 4 • **READY IN** 20 mins

SPECIAL EQUIPMENT Sandwich press or sandwich toaster

① PREPARE THE SANDWICHES

Cut the loaf into 4 x 6–8in (15–20cm) lengths, then slice each in half lengthwise. Lightly coat 4 slices of the bread with mustard and layer each with 1 slice of the roast pork, ham, and cheese. Add a gherkin on top and cover with the remaining slices of bread. Brush the top of each sandwich with butter.

② TOAST AND SERVE

Place the sandwiches in a sandwich press or sandwich toaster, and press down until the cheese has melted and the outside of the bread is crisp. Remove from the press, cut each sandwich diagonally across, and serve hot.

PRESSED CIABATTA WITH GRILLED VEGETABLES

This tasty loaf-sized sandwich is pressed and chilled to squash the fillings together and enhance the flavors. If you'd rather have it warm with the cheese melted, pop it in a toaster oven for a few minutes.

SERVES 4 • **READY IN** 20 mins, plus chilling

INGREDIENTS

- ½ eggplant, cut into ½in (1cm) slices
- 2 zucchini, cut into ½in (1cm) slices
- 4–6 tbsp olive oil
- salt and freshly ground black pepper
- 1 large tomato
- 1 ciabatta loaf
- 2 roasted red bell peppers from a jar, drained, and sliced
- ball of mozzarella, approx. 4½oz (125g), thinly sliced
- handful of basil leaves

1 GRILL THE VEG

Preheat a large grill pan or a broiler to its highest setting. Brush the slices of eggplant and zucchini on both sides with olive oil and season them well. Either grill or broil them for 2–4 minutes each side, until they are charred in places and cooked through. Put them on a large plate in a single layer to cool.

2 SLICE THE TOMATO

Meanwhile, slice about ½in (1cm) off each end of the tomato, reserving these pieces. Slice the remaining tomato as thinly as possible.

3 PREPARE THE CIABATTA

Cut the ciabatta in half, leaving a hinge so you can open it out flat. Drizzle both sides with a little olive oil. Take the ends of the tomato and rub both sides of the bread with the cut sides, to soften and flavor the bread, then discard the tomato ends.

4 ADD THE FILLINGS

Cover one side of the loaf with the roasted peppers and cooled slices of eggplant and zucchini, then top with mozzarella. Sprinkle with the basil, season, then add the tomato.

5 PRESS, CHILL, AND SERVE

Close the loaf and press down on it hard. Wrap it very tightly in plastic wrap, going around it a few times until it is completely covered and compressed. Leave in the fridge with a weight (such as a cutting board and some full cans) on top for at least 4 hours, turning once. Unwrap and slice to serve, or transport in the wrapping and slice at a picnic.

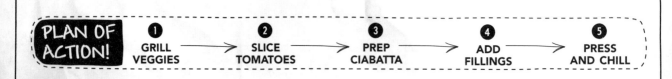

PLAN OF ACTION!

1 GRILL VEGGIES → **2** SLICE TOMATOES → **3** PREP CIABATTA → **4** ADD FILLINGS → **5** PRESS AND CHILL

STILTON RAREBIT WITH PEAR AND WALNUTS

A rarebit is a sophisticated version of cheese on toast, which uses a rich, savory cheese sauce as a topping. Serve with this peppery-sweet, nutty salad for a delicious lunch or filling snack.

SERVES 4 • **READY IN** 20 mins

INGREDIENTS

- 4–8 slices walnut bread
- 1 shallot, finely chopped
- ⅓ cup dry hard cider
- 2 tbsp butter
- 2 tbsp all-purpose flour
- ⅔ cup milk
- 3½oz (100g) Stilton cheese, crumbled
- 1¾oz (50g) Cheddar cheese, grated
- 1 tsp English mustard
- 2 egg yolks
- 2 ripe pears, cored and sliced
- small bunch of watercress
- 2oz (60g) walnuts, broken into pieces
- 1 tbsp balsamic vinegar
- 2 tbsp extra virgin olive oil
- freshly ground black pepper

1 TOAST THE BREAD

Lightly toast the bread; allow 1 or 2 slices per person, depending on the size of the slices.

2 REDUCE THE CIDER

Meanwhile, place the shallot and cider in a small saucepan and simmer over low heat until the cider has almost completely evaporated. Remove from the pan and set aside.

3 MAKE THE CHEESE SAUCE

Wash the pan and add the butter. Place over medium-low heat until melted, then stir in the flour. Cook, stirring, for 1 minute, then remove the pan from the heat and gradually stir in the milk. Return to the heat and cook for 2–3 minutes, or until thickened, stirring constantly. Add the cheeses and stir until melted. Remove from the heat and stir in the mustard, egg yolks, and cooled shallot. Spread the mixture thickly onto each toasted bread slice.

4 BROIL THE TOASTS

Preheat the broiler to its highest setting, then broil the toasts for 2 minutes, or until golden and bubbling.

5 GARNISH AND SERVE

Arrange the pears, watercress, and walnuts on 4 plates, drizzle with a little balsamic vinegar and olive oil, and season with pepper. Place the toasts alongside and serve at once.

PLAN OF ACTION!
1 TOAST BREAD → 2 REDUCE CIDER → 3 MAKE CHEESE SAUCE → 4 BROIL TOASTS → 5 GARNISH AND SERVE

FUSS-FREE FALAFEL

Using a can of chickpeas, instead of dried chickpeas soaked in advance, will give you all the flavor with none of the fuss in this Middle Eastern classic.

MAKES 12 • **READY IN** 20 mins, plus standing
SPECIAL EQUIPMENT Food processor

- 1 x 14oz (400g) can of chickpeas
- 1 tbsp tahini
- 1 garlic clove, crushed
- 1 tsp salt
- 1 tsp ground cumin
- 1 tsp turmeric
- 1 tsp ground coriander
- ½ tsp cayenne pepper

- 2 tbsp finely chopped flat-leaf parsley
- juice of 1 small lemon
- vegetable oil, for frying

TO SERVE
- 4 pitta breads, warmed
- 1 Romaine lettuce, shredded
- 200g pot Greek yogurt
- ½ small cucumber, diced

PREPARE INGREDIENTS

1 DRAIN

TAP

chickpeas

COLANDER

Drain the chickpeas and rinse them under cold running water.

2 ADD

crushed garlic

tahini

salt

cumin

turmeric

ground coriander

cayenne pepper

Add ingredients to food processor bowl.

③ PULSE

MAKE AND SHAPE

FOOD PROCESSOR

Pulse the mixture in a food processor until finely chopped but not puréed.

TRANSFER TO A BOWL, COVER, AND SET ASIDE IN THE FRIDGE FOR AT LEAST 30 MINUTES.

④ SHAPE

Wet your hands and shape the mixture into 12 balls.

⑤ FLATTEN

Press down slightly to flatten.

FRY THE FALAFEL

Heat 2in (5cm) of oil and fry the falafel balls in batches.

SLOTTED SPOON

⑤ FRY

WOK

Fry for 3–4 minutes, or until lightly golden.

⑥ DRAIN

PAPER TOWEL

PITA POCKETS

Mini lamb burgers with arugula and tzatziki

Portobello mushrooms and feta with spinach, red onion, and olives

For the burgers, season ground **lamb** with **cumin**, **salt**, and **pepper**. Form the mixture into patties and broil to your liking.

For the tzatziki, combine ½ cup **Greek yogurt**, 2½oz (75g) roughly chopped **cucumbers**, the juice of 2 **limes**, and ¼ cup chopped **cilantro**.

Use 1 chopped **portobello mushroom** per wrap and cook them in 1 tbsp of **coconut oil** for about 8 minutes.

Chicken and apple salad

Hummus and bean sprouts with cucumber, avocado, and carrot

For the salad, combine 2 shredded **chicken breasts**, 2 chopped **apples**, 2 chopped **celery stalks**, 1¼ cups **Greek yogurt**, and the juice of 1 **lemon**.

- - - - These pita pockets—stuffed with a wide variety of healthy, tasty fillings—are a fast and fun alternative to more run-of-the-mill sandwiches. If you prefer your pita bread warm, simply pop them in the toaster for 30 seconds to 1 minute, until puffed up but not crisp.

Shredded chicken in yellow curry sauce with red onion, avocado, and cilantro

Tuna mayonnaise filling with microgreens and tomatoes

For the filling, combine 7oz (200g) canned **tuna**, 1/4 cup **mayo**, the juice of 1 **lemon**, 1³/₄oz (50g) chopped **gherkins**, and 2¹/₂oz (75g) chopped **red bell peppers**.

For the curry sauce, mix ³/₄ cup **Greek yogurt**, 1/4 cup **coconut milk**, 2 tbsp **yellow curry paste**, and 1 tsp **fish sauce**.

Honey and soy steak with onion and snow peas

Shrimp and avocado with watercress

Pan-fry **steak** strips and sliced **onion** in **sesame oil** and coat with 3 tbsp each of **honey** and **soy sauce**, and 1 tbsp **sesame seeds**.

GAZPACHO

This chilled, no-cook Spanish soup is lovely for a hot day, or when you need a taste of summer! The vegetables are the stars of the show, so use the freshest you can find—the no-cook approach will celebrate their ripe flavor.

SERVES 4 • **READY IN** 15 mins, plus chilling
SPECIAL EQUIPMENT Food processor or blender

❶ PEEL AND CHOP THE TOMATOES

Bring a pan of water to a boil. Place the tomatoes in a heatproof bowl, pour over enough boiling water to cover, and leave for 20 seconds, or until the skins split. Drain and cool under cold running water. Gently peel off the skins and cut the tomatoes in half, then seed and chop the flesh.

❷ PROCESS INGREDIENTS

Place the tomato flesh, cucumber, red bell pepper, garlic, and vinegar in a food processor or blender. Season to taste and process until smooth. Pour in the oil and process again. Dilute with a little cold water or a few ice cubes if too thick. Transfer the soup to a serving bowl, cover with plastic wrap, and chill.

❸ PREPARE THE GARNISHES

When ready to serve, finely chop the extra cucumber and red bell pepper. Place the cucumber, bell pepper, and egg yolk and white in individual bowls and arrange on the table, along with a bottle of olive oil. Ladle the soup into bowls and serve, letting each diner add their own garnish. If the soup hasn't had enough time to chill properly, add an ice cube or two to each bowl.

To make a more **substantial meal**, add cubes of stale bread soaked in olive oil and a dash of sherry vinegar at step 2.
For a seafood twist, try adding 4oz (115g) small cooked, peeled shrimp (thawed if frozen) into the serving bowls at step 3.

INGREDIENTS

2¼lb (1kg) tomatoes, plus extra to serve

1 small cucumber, peeled and finely chopped, plus extra to serve

1 small red bell pepper, seeded and chopped, plus extra to serve

2 garlic cloves, crushed

¼ cup sherry vinegar

salt and freshly ground black pepper

½ cup extra virgin olive oil, plus extra to serve

1 hard-boiled egg, white and yolk separated and chopped, to serve

SWEET POTATO SOUP

This sophisticated soup is rich and velvety, and can be ready in minutes. The crispy croutons add a satisfying crunch and make this hearty dish even more substantial.

SERVES 4–6 • **READY IN** 20 mins
SPECIAL EQUIPMENT hand-held blender

- 5 tbsp olive oil
- 1 onion, chopped
- 1 leek, white part only, chopped
- 1 celery stalk, chopped
- 1lb 2oz (500g) sweet potatoes, peeled and cut into 1in (3cm) cubes

- 2½ cups vegetable or chicken stock
- ½ tbsp chopped sage leaves
- salt and freshly ground black pepper
- 4 slices of day-old white bread, crusts removed and cut into ½in (1cm) dice
- 2 tbsp unsalted butter

PREPARE THE SOUP

1 SOFTEN

onion   leek   celery

olive oil

Heat 3 tbsp of oil and cook the veggies for 5 minutes until softened but not browned.

2 ADD

liquid stock

sweet potato   sage

salt   pepper

Bring to a boil.

WHILE THE SOUP IS SIMMERING, PREPARE THE CROUTONS.

3 SIMMMER

SAUCEPAN LID

Reduce the heat to a gentle simmer, cover, and cook for 10 minutes or until the sweet potato is tender.

MAKE THE CROUTONS

4 FRY

WOODEN SPOON

bread dice

LARGE FRYING PAN

olive oil and unsalted butter

Heat the oil and butter until hot, add the bread dice, then fry, stirring constantly.

SLOTTED SPOON

PAPER TOWELS

5 DRAIN

Fry the croutons for 10 minutes or until golden, then remove with a slotted spoon and drain on paper towels.

BLEND AND SERVE

6 BLEND

salt

pepper

HAND-HELD BLENDER

Blend the soup until completely smooth, then check the seasoning.

7 SERVE

LADLE

croutons

Ladle the soup into serving bowls and garnish with the croutons.

SOPA AL CUARTO DE HORA

The Spanish name of this dish translates as "15-minute soup" because that's how long it takes to cook! It's ideal for when you want a nourishing meal in no time. Why not serve this flavorful broth with toasted bread for dunking?

SERVES 4 • **READY IN** 20 mins

- -

1 SIMMER THE RICE

In a large pan, bring the broth, rice, and ham to a boil. Reduce the heat and simmer for 15 minutes, or until the rice is nearly tender.

2 ADD THE EGGS AND HERBS

Add the eggs and simmer for another minute. Remove from the heat, then stir in the parsley and mint, if using. Serve piping hot.

TIP – You can cut down the preparation time by using pre-cooked leftover rice, or by replacing the rice with soup pasta, such as vermicelli or ditalini.

INGREDIENTS

3½ cups hot chicken or beef broth, fresh or from powdered stock

2 tbsp rice

¼ cup diced Serrano ham

2 eggs, hard-boiled and chopped

1 tbsp finely chopped flat-leaf parsley

1 tbsp finely chopped mint (optional)

SUMMER PEA, MINT, AND QUINOA SOUP

This light and creamy chilled soup is enhanced by the addition of protein-packed quinoa and nutty-flavored almond milk. Quick and easy to prepare, it makes the perfect summer lunch.

SERVES 4 • **READY IN** 20–25 mins, plus cooling
SPECIAL EQUIPMENT Food processor

INGREDIENTS

- ½ cup uncooked quinoa
- 2 avocados, pitted
- 1lb 2oz (500g) frozen peas
- ¾oz (20g) chopped mint, plus extra to garnish
- 3½ cups unsweetened almond milk

1 PREPARE THE QUINOA

Rinse the quinoa under running water, drain, and place in a lidded saucepan. Cover with 1 cup of water and bring to a boil.

2 COOK THE QUINOA

Reduce the heat to a simmer, cover, and cook for 15–20 minutes, or until almost all the liquid has been absorbed and the quinoa is fluffy. Remove from the heat, drain any remaining water, and set aside to cool.

3 BLEND THE AVOCADOS, PEAS, MINT, AND MILK

While the quinoa is cooking, scoop out the flesh from the avocados and place in a food processor. Add the peas, mint, and half the milk and pulse until smooth. Then add the remaining milk and process until fully blended.

4 DIVIDE AND SERVE

Divide the soup equally between four soup bowls. Top with equal quantities of the cooled quinoa. Garnish with some mint and serve immediately.

> **You can substitute** cow's milk for the almond milk, if you like.

PLAN OF ACTION!
1 PREPARE QUINOA → **2** COOK QUINOA → **3** BLEND INGREDIENTS → **4** DIVIDE AND SERVE

PARMESAN BROTH

This elegant pick-me-up enjoyed in Rome—where it is known as *stracciatella alla romana*—is made by swirling raw egg beaten with grated Parmesan cheese into boiling chicken broth.

SERVES 4-5 • **READY IN** 20 mins

INGREDIENTS

- 7 cups hot chicken stock
- salt
- 4–5 eggs
- 2 tbsp finely grated Parmesan cheese
- 1 tsp freshly grated nutmeg
- grated zest of 1 lemon
- 2 tbsp finely chopped flat-leaf parsley

1 REDUCE THE STOCK

In a large saucepan, bring the chicken stock to a boil and let simmer until reduced by one-third. Season to taste with salt.

2 WHISK THE EGGS AND CHEESE TOGETHER

In a bowl, whisk the eggs with the Parmesan, nutmeg, and lemon zest, until well-blended.

3 COMBINE THE STOCK AND EGG MIXTURE

Reduce the heat to a steady simmer and whisk in the egg mixture. Continue to whisk for another 1–2 minutes as the egg forms fine pasta-like threads.

4 TASTE, GARNISH, AND SERVE

Taste the broth and add more cheese and seasoning, if you like. Garnish with parsley.

You could also add diced prosciutto, finely chopped parsley, and a few scraps of seeded peperoncino pepper to the soup, if you like.

PLAN OF ACTION! 1 REDUCE STOCK → 2 WHISK EGGS AND CHEESE → 3 COMBINE STOCK AND EGG MIXTURE → 4 TASTE, GARNISH, AND SERVE

SALAD-IN-A-JAR

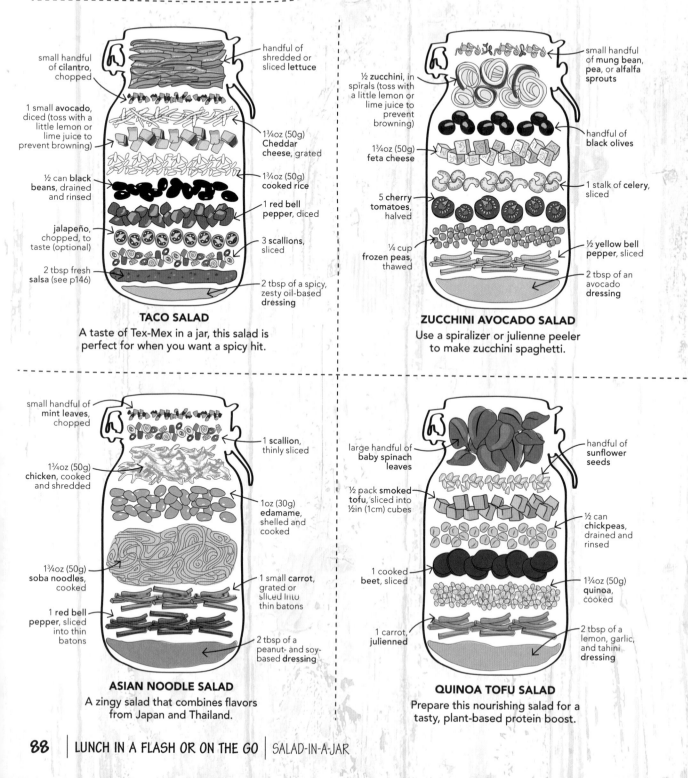

TACO SALAD

small handful of **cilantro**, chopped

1 small **avocado**, diced (toss with a little lemon or lime juice to prevent browning)

½ can **black beans**, drained and rinsed

jalapeño, chopped, to taste (optional)

2 tbsp fresh **salsa** (see p146)

handful of shredded or sliced **lettuce**

1¾oz (50g) **Cheddar cheese**, grated

1¾oz (50g) **cooked rice**

1 **red bell pepper**, diced

3 **scallions**, sliced

2 tbsp of a spicy, zesty oil-based **dressing**

A taste of Tex-Mex in a jar, this salad is perfect for when you want a spicy hit.

ZUCCHINI AVOCADO SALAD

½ **zucchini**, in spirals (toss with a little lemon or lime juice to prevent browning)

1¾oz (50g) **feta cheese**

5 **cherry tomatoes**, halved

¼ cup **frozen peas**, thawed

small handful of **mung bean, pea, or alfalfa sprouts**

handful of **black olives**

1 stalk of **celery**, sliced

½ **yellow bell pepper**, sliced

2 tbsp of an avocado **dressing**

Use a spiralizer or julienne peeler to make zucchini spaghetti.

ASIAN NOODLE SALAD

small handful of **mint leaves**, chopped

1¾oz (50g) **chicken**, cooked and shredded

1¾oz (50g) **soba noodles**, cooked

1 **red bell pepper**, sliced into thin batons

1 **scallion**, thinly sliced

1oz (30g) **edamame**, shelled and cooked

1 small **carrot**, grated or sliced into thin batons

2 tbsp of a peanut- and soy-based **dressing**

A zingy salad that combines flavors from Japan and Thailand.

QUINOA TOFU SALAD

large handful of **baby spinach leaves**

½ pack **smoked tofu**, sliced into ½in (1cm) cubes

1 cooked **beet**, sliced

1 **carrot**, julienned

handful of **sunflower seeds**

½ can **chickpeas**, drained and rinsed

1¾oz (50g) **quinoa**, cooked

2 tbsp of a lemon, garlic, and tahini **dressing**

Prepare this nourishing salad for a tasty, plant-based protein boost.

A speedy salad-in-a-jar makes an easy, transportable lunch. Layering the ingredients in the right order will prevent the dressing from spreading and making the greens soggy. When you're ready to eat, simply tip the jar upside down and shake to combine. See pages 90–91 for dressing ideas.

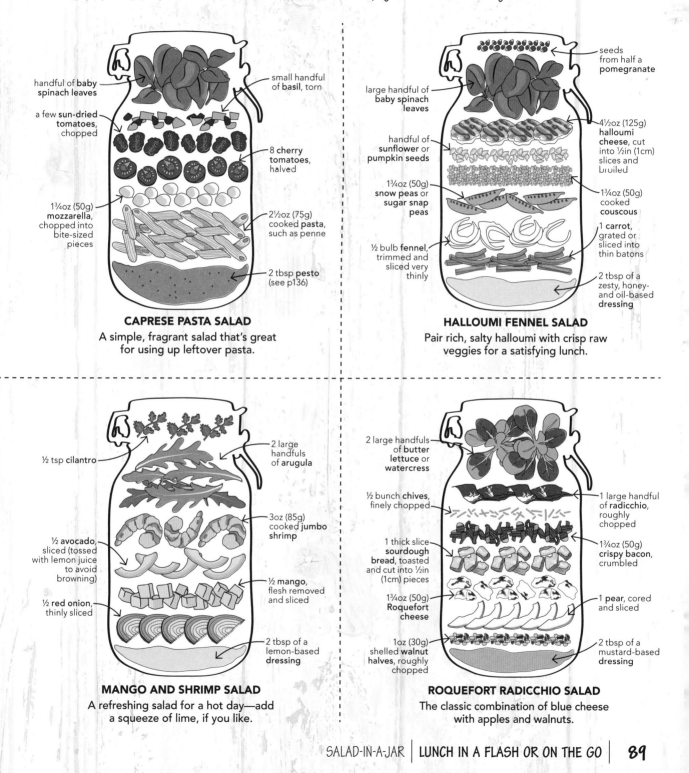

handful of **baby spinach leaves**

small handful of **basil**, torn

a few **sun-dried tomatoes**, chopped

8 **cherry tomatoes**, halved

1¾oz (50g) **mozzarella**, chopped into bite-sized pieces

2½ (75g) cooked **pasta**, such as penne

2 tbsp **pesto** (see p136)

CAPRESE PASTA SALAD
A simple, fragrant salad that's great for using up leftover pasta.

seeds from half a **pomegranate**

large handful of **baby spinach leaves**

handful of **sunflower** or **pumpkin seeds**

1¾oz (50g) **snow peas** or **sugar snap peas**

½ bulb **fennel**, trimmed and sliced very thinly

4½oz (125g) **halloumi cheese**, cut into ½in (1cm) slices and broiled

1¾oz (50g) cooked **couscous**

1 **carrot**, grated or sliced into thin batons

2 tbsp of a zesty, honey- and oil-based **dressing**

HALLOUMI FENNEL SALAD
Pair rich, salty halloumi with crisp raw veggies for a satisfying lunch.

½ tsp **cilantro**

2 large handfuls of **arugula**

½ **avocado**, sliced (tossed with lemon juice to avoid browning)

½ **red onion**, thinly sliced

3oz (85g) cooked **jumbo shrimp**

½ **mango**, flesh removed and sliced

2 tbsp of a lemon-based **dressing**

MANGO AND SHRIMP SALAD
A refreshing salad for a hot day—add a squeeze of lime, if you like.

2 large handfuls of **butter lettuce** or **watercress**

½ bunch **chives**, finely chopped

1 thick slice **sourdough bread**, toasted and cut into ½in (1cm) pieces

1¾oz (50g) **Roquefort cheese**

1oz (30g) shelled **walnut halves**, roughly chopped

1 large handful of **radicchio**, roughly chopped

1¾oz (50g) **crispy bacon**, crumbled

1 **pear**, cored and sliced

2 tbsp of a mustard-based **dressing**

ROQUEFORT RADICCHIO SALAD
The classic combination of blue cheese with apples and walnuts.

WHEEL OF SALAD DRESSINGS

Use this wheel to experiment with your own dressing ideas and give any salad a speedy makeover. To test your combo, dip in a piece of lettuce, shaking off the excess. This will give you a better idea of how it tastes than by dipping in a finger—and if it's not quite right you won't ruin the whole salad!

MAKE YOUR DRESSING

Most dressings are based on a ratio of 3 parts oil to 1 part acid (vinegar or citrus), plus additional flavorings, which act as "emulsifiers" to help the oil and vinegar combine and so coat the salad evenly. Add fruit, veggies, or seaonings to taste. (See the center of the wheel for ratios.)

- - - - - - - - - - - - - - - - - - -

①

CHOOSE YOUR OIL OR FAT BASE
Add it to the blender.

②

CHOOSE YOUR ACID
Pop in a vinegar or other acidic ingredient.

③

ADD A FLAVORING
To help the dressing emulsify.

④

ADD VEGGIES, FRUIT, OR SEASONINGS
If you wish!

Why not try parsley, basil, mint, rosemary, tarragon, oregano, cilantro, dill, chives, or thyme?

① OIL OR FAT BASE

- PEANUT OIL
- HEMP SEED OIL
- COCONUT OIL
- CANOLA OIL
- SUNFLOWER OIL
- EXTRA VIRGIN OLIVE OIL
- SOUR CREAM
- MAYONNAISE
- GREEK YOGURT
- TAHINI

3 PARTS

½ PART

④ VEGGIES, FRUIT, AND SEASONINGS

- RED PEPPER FLAKES
- CITRUS ZEST
  lemon, lime, grapefruit, orange
- SUN-DRIED TOMATOES
  finely chopped
- OLIVES
  finely chopped
- TOMATOES
  finely chopped
- FRESH OR DRIED HERBS
  finely chopped
- JALAPEÑOS
  finely sliced
- BERRIES OR BERRY COULIS
  raspberries, blackberries, blueberries, strawberries
- MANGO
  peeled, pit removed, and finely chopped

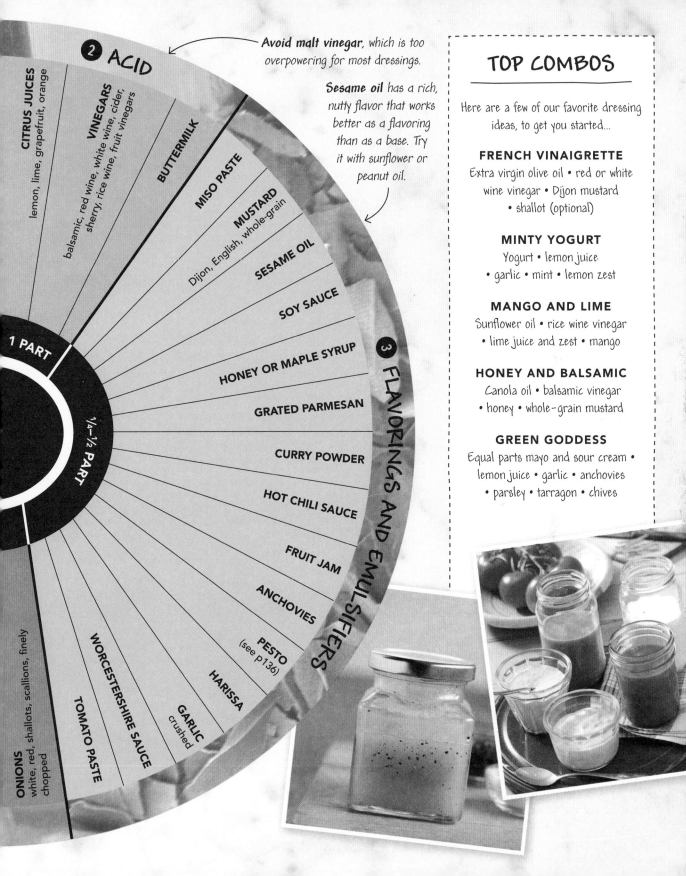

2 ACID

Avoid malt vinegar, which is too overpowering for most dressings.

Sesame oil has a rich, nutty flavor that works better as a flavoring than as a base. Try it with sunflower or peanut oil.

CITRUS JUICES
lemon, lime, grapefruit, orange

VINEGARS
balsamic, red wine, white wine, cider, sherry, rice wine, fruit vinegars

BUTTERMILK

MISO PASTE

MUSTARD
Dijon, English, whole-grain

SESAME OIL

SOY SAUCE

HONEY OR MAPLE SYRUP

GRATED PARMESAN

CURRY POWDER

HOT CHILI SAUCE

FRUIT JAM

ANCHOVIES

PESTO
(see p136)

HARISSA

GARLIC
crushed

WORCESTERSHIRE SAUCE

TOMATO PASTE

ONIONS
white, red, shallots, scallions, finely chopped

1 PART

¼–½ PART

3 FLAVORINGS AND EMULSIFIERS

TOP COMBOS

Here are a few of our favorite dressing ideas, to get you started...

FRENCH VINAIGRETTE
Extra virgin olive oil • red or white wine vinegar • Dijon mustard • shallot (optional)

MINTY YOGURT
Yogurt • lemon juice • garlic • mint • lemon zest

MANGO AND LIME
Sunflower oil • rice wine vinegar • lime juice and zest • mango

HONEY AND BALSAMIC
Canola oil • balsamic vinegar • honey • whole-grain mustard

GREEN GODDESS
Equal parts mayo and sour cream • lemon juice • garlic • anchovies • parsley • tarragon • chives

WALDORF SALAD

Created at the Waldorf Astoria Hotel in New York, this creamy and crunchy salad has been a favorite for over 100 years. It goes well with grilled chicken if you need something a bit more filling.

SERVES 4 • **READY IN** 15 mins

INGREDIENTS

- 2 large apples
- 4 celery stalks, thinly sliced
- 25 red seedless grapes, halved
- 2 tbsp toasted and crushed walnuts
- ¼ cup mayonnaise
- juice of 1 lemon, plus extra for squeezing
- salt and freshly ground black pepper
- 2 hearts of Romaine lettuce

1 DICE THE APPLES

Remove the cores of the apples using a corer. Then, using a sharp knife, cut the apples into slices of an even thickness. Stack the slices, a few at a time, and cut lengthwise through the pile and then crosswise, making equal-sized cubes.

2 DRESS AND TOSS THE SALAD

Put the apples, celery, grapes, and walnuts in a bowl. Add the mayonnaise and lemon juice and toss well to combine. Season with salt and pepper to taste.

3 ADD LETTUCE AND SERVE

Roughly chop the lettuce and divide between 4 plates. Serve the fruit and nut mixture on each bed of lettuce with a squeeze of lemon.

PLAN OF ACTION!

1 DICE APPLES → **2** DRESS AND TOSS SALAD → **3** ADD LETTUCE AND SERVE

TOMATO, MOZZARELLA, AND RED ONION SALAD

10 MINS OR LESS!

Versatile and easy to prepare, this simple salad bursts with vibrant colors and delicious Italian flavors. You can pull this together in minutes—serve it with ciabatta to soak up the juices, if you like.

SERVES 4 • **READY IN** 10 mins

INGREDIENTS

- 8 ripe plum tomatoes, sliced
- 6 cherry tomatoes, halved
- 1 small red onion, peeled and sliced
- handful of basil leaves, torn
- extra virgin olive oil, to drizzle
- salt and freshly ground black pepper
- 2 handfuls of wild arugula leaves
- balsamic vinegar, to drizzle
- 2 balls of mozzarella, torn into pieces

1 DRESS THE INGREDIENTS

Place the tomatoes, onion, and half of the basil leaves in a bowl. Drizzle with plenty of olive oil, season with salt and pepper to taste, and toss through.

2 COMBINE, SEASON, AND SERVE

Arrange the arugula leaves on a serving platter and drizzle with a little oil and balsamic vinegar. Season and spoon the tomato and basil mixture over the top. Add the torn mozzarella. Scatter with the remaining basil leaves, and drizzle again with a little oil and balsamic vinegar. Serve immediately.

> **Why not** toss this salad with pasta with some garlic oil for a simple summery lunch? Add the arugula at the end to prevent it from wilting.

PLAN OF ACTION! 1 DRESS INGREDIENTS ⟶ 2 COMBINE AND SERVE

JEWELED COUSCOUS IN A JIFFY

A stylish Middle Eastern–inspired salad that you can bring together without any cooking at all. Why not make it the night before and pack in a lunchbox for a weekday lunch? It's cheaper and much tastier than a supermarket sandwich.

SERVES 4–6 • **READY IN** 12 mins

1 MAKE THE STOCK

Bring a small saucepan of water to a boil. Put the couscous into a bowl and drizzle in ½ tablespoon of olive oil. Rub it into the couscous, scatter with the powdered vegetable stock (if using), and mix it in.

2 SOAK THE COUSCOUS

Pour in 2 cups of boiling water (if using powdered stock) or hot vegetable stock, and stir briefly. The liquid should just cover the couscous. Immediately seal with plastic wrap.

3 REST, TEST, AND COOL

Leave for 5 minutes, then test the grains, which should be nearly soft, and all the water soaked in. Fluff the couscous with a fork and let it cool, fluffing it occasionally to separate the grains.

4 TOAST THE PINE NUTS

Meanwhile dry-fry the pine nuts in a non-stick frying pan over medium heat, stirring, until they color. Be careful, as they can burn quickly. Set aside to cool.

5 MIX IT ALL UP

Toss together the cooled couscous, pine nuts, apricots, and cilantro. Mix in the extra virgin olive oil and lemon juice and season to taste. Scatter with the pomegranate seeds to serve.

1 MAKE STOCK → **2** SOAK COUSCOUS → **3** REST AND TEST → **4** TOAST PINE NUTS → **5** MIX IT UP

INGREDIENTS

2 cups couscous

1½ tbsp olive oil

1 tbsp powdered vegetable stock or 2 cups hot vegetable stock

1¾oz (50g) pine nuts

3½oz (100g) dried apricots, finely chopped

large handful of cilantro, finely chopped

4½ tbsp extra virgin olive oil

juice of 1 large lemon

salt and freshly ground black pepper

2 or 3 tbsp pomegranate seeds, to serve

INGREDIENTS

12oz (350g) filet steak, or flank steak

7oz (200g) rice vermicelli or mung bean noodles

9oz (250g) green papaya or green mango, peeled, seeded, and cut into matchsticks or coarsely grated

¼ cup roasted unsalted peanuts, coarsely chopped

FOR THE DRESSING

1 tsp lemongrass purée

1 tsp finely grated fresh ginger

2 tbsp chopped cilantro

2 tbsp Vietnamese *nuoc mam* or Thai fish sauce

2 tbsp chopped mint

juice of 2 limes

1 tsp brown sugar

2 fresh red chiles, seeded and finely chopped

PLAN OF ACTION!

❶ **BROIL BEEF** → ❷ **SOAK NOODLES** → ❸ **MAKE DRESSING**

GREEN PAPAYA, BEEF, AND NOODLE SALAD

A vibrant, Vietnamese-inspired noodle salad, this meal makes for a refreshing lunch. Green papayas are underripe fruit that are featured in many Southeast Asian salads—if you can't find papaya, green mango works just as well.

SERVES 4 • **READY IN** 20 mins, plus resting

1 TRIM AND BROIL THE BEEF
Preheat the broiler to high. Trim any fat from the steak and broil for 3–4 minutes on each side, or until browned but still pink in the center. Set aside for at least 15 minutes before slicing into thin strips.

2 SOAK THE NOODLES
Soak the vermicelli in boiling water until softened, or as directed on the package. Drain, rinse in cold water, then cut into manageable lengths with kitchen scissors. Set aside.

3 MAKE THE DRESSING
Mix together the lemongrass, ginger, cilantro, fish sauce, mint, lime juice, sugar, and chiles.

4 TOSS TOGETHER AND SERVE
Pile the noodles, papaya, and steak into a serving dish and add the dressing. Toss lightly together and scatter with peanuts before serving.

TIP – If you want, you can broil the steak several hours in advance and slice it just before adding to the salad.

This salad appears in many variations across Vietnam, Thailand, and Cambodia. Why not try eating it Thai-style? Use grilled chicken in place of the beef, and sticky white rice instead of noodles.

SPICY ASIAN CHICKEN SALAD

This colorful salad is tasty as well as healthy, and requires very little cooking. You can reserve some of the salad, undressed, for tomorrow's lunch; toss with the dressing at the last minute to prevent wilting.

SERVES 4–6 • **READY IN** 20 mins

INGREDIENTS

- 14oz (400g) boneless, skinless chicken breasts
- salt
- ¼ cup fresh lime juice
- 4 tsp Thai fish sauce
- 1 tbsp granulated sugar
- pinch of red pepper flakes (optional)
- 1 little gem lettuce, shredded
- 3½oz (100g) beansprouts
- 1 large carrot, shaved using a vegetable peeler
- 6in (15cm) piece of cucumber, seeded and finely sliced
- ½ red bell pepper, finely sliced
- ½ yellow bell pepper, finely sliced
- approx. 15 cherry tomatoes, halved
- small handful of mint leaves, chopped
- small handful of cilantro leaves, chopped
- 1¾oz (50g) salted peanuts, chopped (optional)

❶ POACH THE CHICKEN

Poach the chicken in a large saucepan in plenty of simmering salted water or chicken stock for 7–10 minutes, depending on thickness, until cooked through. Let cool, then thinly slice.

❷ MAKE THE DRESSING

Whisk the lime juice, fish sauce, sugar, a pinch of salt, and the red pepper flakes (if using) together, until the sugar dissolves.

❸ TOSS TOGETHER AND SERVE

Mix together the salad vegetables, most of the herbs, and the chicken. Mix in the dressing and scatter with the remaining herbs and the peanuts (if using), to serve.

TIP – To save time, prepare the vegetables while the chicken is poaching. To speed-cut cherry tomatoes, place several on a small plate, invert a second small plate on top and, holding the top plate in place, use a sharp knife to slice between the plates and through the tomatoes, making sure you cut away from yourself.

PLAN OF ACTION! ❶ POACH CHICKEN → ❷ MAKE DRESSING → ❸ TOSS AND SERVE

BULGUR WHEAT WITH MIXED BELL PEPPERS AND GOAT CHEESE

Sweet, crunchy peppers and creamy goat cheese are a winning combination. Bulgur wheat is a great staple for your cupboard— it's a source of fiber and protein, and very easy to prepare.

SERVES 4 • **READY IN** 15 mins

INGREDIENTS

- 1¼ cups fine bulgur wheat
- 1¼ cups hot vegetable stock
- salt and freshly ground black pepper
- 1 bunch of scallions, finely chopped
- 1 orange bell pepper, seeded and diced
- 1 yellow bell pepper, seeded and diced
- pinch of mild paprika
- handful of fresh mint leaves, finely chopped
- juice of 1 lemon
- 4½oz (125g) soft goat cheese, crumbled
- extra virgin olive oil, for drizzling

1 SOAK THE BULGUR WHEAT

Put the bulgur wheat in a large bowl, and pour in enough stock to just cover the bulgur. Leave for 10 minutes, then stir with a fork to fluff up the grains. Season with salt and pepper to taste.

2 ADD THE VEGGIES AND CHEESE

Add the scallions, orange and yellow bell peppers, paprika, mint, and lemon juice, and stir well. Taste, and season again if needed. To serve, top with the goat cheese and a generous drizzle of olive oil.

> **You could use**
> couscous instead of bulgur wheat and feta instead of goat cheese, if you like. For the couscous, pour over enough hot stock just to cover the couscous, then cover the bowl with plastic wrap and leave for 5 minutes before fluffing up with a fork.

PLAN OF ACTION! → **1 SOAK BULGUR WHEAT** → **2 ADD VEGGIES AND CHEESE**

BEAN BURGERS

These bean burgers are a tasty, low-fat alternative to the traditional beef burger, and can be put together in no time! Omit the anchovies to make them vegetarian.

MAKES 6 • **READY IN** 20 mins

SPECIAL EQUIPMENT Food processor

- 1 x 14oz (400g) can aduki beans, drained and rinsed
- 1 x 14oz (400g) can chickpeas, drained and rinsed
- 1 onion, roughly chopped
- 6 salted anchovies in olive oil, drained
- 1 tbsp whole-grain mustard
- 2 eggs
- salt and freshly ground black pepper

- 2–3 tbsp all-purpose flour, plus extra for dusting
- 2–3 tbsp vegetable or sunflower oil, for frying

TO SERVE
- 2 burger buns, toasted
- crisp lettuce, such as little gem
- ketchup

PREPARE THE BEANS

1 RINSE

chickpeas

aduki beans

COLANDER

Drain and rinse the beans in a colander.

2 PULSE BEANS

Give the chickpeas and aduki beans a quick pulse or two until they're broken up.

FOOD PROCESSOR

If you don't have a food processor, you can use a potato masher to crush the beans to a rough paste before stirring in the remaining ingredients. Make sure you chop the anchovies and whisk the eggs before adding.

ADD THE OTHER INGREDIENTS

3 ADD FLAVORINGS

onions anchovies mustard

Pulse again ...

4 ADD EGGS

eggs salt pepper

... and again ...

5 ADD FLOUR

... and again!

FORM AND FRY

6 FORM

Form into patties.

7 COOK

Heat the oil and cook in batches of 2 or 3 over medium heat for 3–4 minutes on each side, or until golden.

ASSEMBLE THE BURGERS

8 STACK

bun

ketchup

bean burger

lettuce

bun

TUNA AND ARTICHOKE SALAD

A hearty meal-in-one salad, this dish is enhanced by a few pantry ingredients and some fresh green beans. It's packed with flavor and pretty enough to share! Prepare ahead for a tasty weekday packed lunch.

SERVES 4 • **READY IN** 20 mins

- -

1 **BOIL THE PASTA AND BEANS**

Bring a large pan of water to a boil and cook the pasta according to the package instructions, adding the green beans 4–5 minutes before the end of the cooking time. Drain and rinse under cold running water until the pasta is cold. Drain well and place in a serving dish. Add the tuna, cannellini beans, sun-dried tomatoes, and artichokes and stir well.

2 **MAKE THE DRESSING**

Place 3 tablespoons of the oil from the sun-dried tomatoes and 3 tablespoons of the oil from the drained artichokes in a small bowl. Stir in the lemon zest and juice, mustard, and seasoning.

3 **DRESS THE SALAD**

Pour the lemon-mustard dressing over the pasta. Add the herbs and toss well to coat. Cover and chill until ready to serve.

TIP – Save any remaining oil from the sun-dried tomatoes and artichokes. As well as being delicious in salad dressings, the oils add extra flavor when pan-frying vegetables.

For a vegetarian version, omit the tuna and add a 9oz (250g) jar of roasted bell pepper strips instead, and a handful of rinsed capers or green olives.

INGREDIENTS

7¾oz (220g) quick-cook pasta shapes

3½oz (100g) thin green beans, trimmed and halved if long

7oz can of tuna in spring water, drained and flaked

14oz can of cannellini beans, drained and rinsed

10 sun-dried tomatoes in oil, drained and roughly chopped (oil reserved)

1 x 9oz (250g) jar artichoke hearts in oil, drained (oil reserved)

finely grated zest and juice of 1 lemon

1 tsp whole-grain mustard

salt and freshly ground black pepper

3 tbsp chopped flat-leaf parsley leaves

leaves from 3 sprigs of basil, torn

DO-IT-YOURSELF SUSHI

TO MAKE THE SUSHI RICE...

1 Rinse ¾ cup of shari or sushi rice under running water.

2 Add to a saucepan with 1 cup of water.

3 Bring to a boil, stir, lower the heat to medium, then cover.

4 Let simmer for 6–8 minutes, or until the water has been absorbed.

5 Transfer the cooked rice to a mixing bowl.

6 Mix in ½ cup rice vinegar, 1 tbsp sugar, and a pinch of salt.

TO MAKE THE SUSHI ROLLS...

1 Place a sheet of nori (seaweed) on a bamboo mat. Cover the nori in a ¼in (5mm) layer of cooled sushi rice, pressing it down with your fingertips. Leave uncovered a ½in (1cm) strip along the top of the nori, farthest away from you.

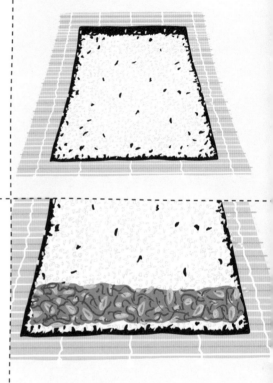

2 Add a layer of filling in a strip along the bottom of the nori, closest to you.

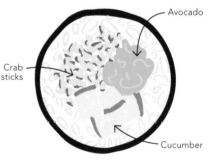

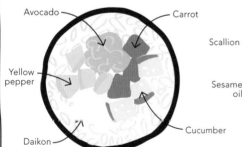

GARDEN ROLL

Fill with 1 **avocado**, sliced, 1¾oz (50g) each of **carrot** and **cucumber** matchsticks, 1 **yellow bell pepper**, finely chopped, and 1 **daikon**, peeled and thinly sliced.

SPICY TUNA ROLL

Fill with 2½oz (75g) fresh **sashimi tuna**, finely chopped, combined with 1 tbsp **hot chili sauce**, a dash of **sesame oil**, and 1 tbsp **scallion**, sliced.

CALIFORNIA ROLL

Fill with 1 **avocado**, sliced, 1¾oz (50g) **cucumber** cut into matchsticks, and 2 **crab sticks**, shredded.

These delicious sushi rolls are surprisingly quick and easy to make—and they're ideal for lunch on the go. Follow the basic rice and rolling technique, then choose from the fillings at the bottom of the page. If you prepare the filling ingredients while the rice is cooking, the sushi will be ready in 20 minutes. Makes 1 good serving.

3 Tightly roll the bamboo mat, starting from the end closest to you. Tuck in the edge of the nori, but lift the mat up as you roll it forward. Wet the uncovered end of the nori with rice wine vinegar and, as you finish the roll, press to seal.

4 Trim the edges of the roll so they are straight and neat, then slice the roll into 8 equal pieces.

TO SERVE...

Serve the sushi rolls with **pickled ginger**, and **soy sauce** and **wasabi** to dip.

You can buy prepared **pickled ginger**, but if you have a little extra time it's fun to make your own. Simply toss 8oz (225g) **young fresh ginger**, peeled and finely sliced, with 1 tbsp **salt**. Leave for 30 minutes. Mix together 1 cup **rice vinegar** and 3 tbsp **sugar**. Bring to a boil, then pour over the salted ginger. Let cool before serving, or refrigerate for up to two weeks.

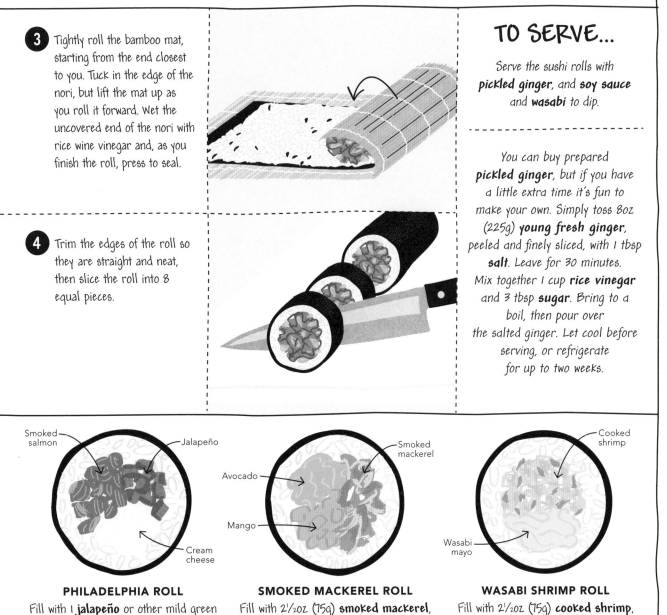

Smoked salmon · Jalapeño · Cream cheese

Avocado · Smoked mackerel · Mango

Cooked shrimp · Wasabi mayo

PHILADELPHIA ROLL
Fill with 1 **jalapeño** or other mild green chile pepper, seeded and finely chopped, 3 tbsp **cream cheese**, and 1³/₄oz (50g) **smoked salmon**.

SMOKED MACKEREL ROLL
Fill with 2¹/₂oz (75g) **smoked mackerel**, shredded, 1³/₄oz (50g) **fresh mango**, sliced, and 1 **avocado**, sliced.

WASABI SHRIMP ROLL
Fill with 2¹/₂oz (75g) **cooked shrimp**, chopped, and 3 tbsp **wasabi mayo** (make by combining mayonnaise with a little wasabi paste, to taste).

SQUASH FRITTATA

This easy-to-prepare frittata is packed with the goodness of butternut squash and spinach, and makes for a quick, delicious, and wholesome meal.

SERVES 2 • **READY IN** 20–30 mins

- 1 small butternut squash, about 1lb 2oz (500g), seeded and diced
- 2 tbsp olive oil
- pat of butter
- 1 small onion, diced
- 7oz (200g) spinach
- 4½oz (125g) soft goat cheese

- 4 sun-dried tomatoes in oil, drained and cut into small pieces
- 2 tbsp grated Parmesan cheese
- grated nutmeg
- 2 tbsp chopped tarragon
- 6 eggs, beaten
- salt and freshly ground black pepper

COOK THE FILLING

1 BLANCH

SAUCEPAN

butternut squash

boiling water

Blanch (briefly boil) the butternut squash for 2–4 minutes, until slightly softened.

2 DRAIN

COLANDER

Thoroughly drain the squash.

3 SOFTEN

onions

WOODEN SPOON

butternut squash

oil and butter

LARGE NON-STICK FRYING PAN

Heat the oil and butter, add the onions, and cook for 3 minutes. Then add the squash and cook for 2 minutes.

4 WILT

If you like, use Swiss chard or bok choy in place of the spinach.

spinach

Add the spinach and cook for 2 minutes to wilt. Simmer for 1–2 minutes more to drive off any liquid, stirring gently.

WHILE THE SPINACH IS SIMMERING, SEASON THE BEATEN EGGS AND PREHEAT THE BROILER TO ITS HIGHEST SETTING.

5 ADD FLAVORINGS

goat cheese

sun-dried tomatoes

tarragon

nutmeg

Parmesan

Add the goat cheese and tomatoes and spread them out evenly. Sprinkle over the Parmesan, nutmeg, and tarragon.

COOK THE EGGS THEN BROIL

FRYING PAN LID

Lift and stir the eggs.

6 ADD EGGS

Cook the eggs until just beginning to set, then cover and cook for 5 more minutes.

Remove the lid, transfer the pan to the broiler, and cook for 3–4 minutes to brown the top. Cut into wedges and serve.

7 BROIL

QUICK FRITTATA

A fancy version of cheesy scrambled eggs with tomato, this dish, known as *kayiana* in Greek cuisine, is the ultimate comfort food—ideal for a warming, filling lunch in no time.

SERVES 4-5 • **READY IN** 20 mins

INGREDIENTS

- ¼ cup olive oil
- 2 large ripe, firm tomatoes, thickly sliced
- 1 garlic clove, chopped
- 3½oz (100g) mozzarella or taleggio cheese, diced
- 6 large eggs
- 1 tbsp finely chopped dill
- salt and freshly ground black pepper

❶ COOK THE TOMATOES

Heat the oil in a small frying pan. Spread the tomato slices in an even layer over the surface and sprinkle with the garlic. Cook over low heat until the tomatoes are soft and slightly dry. Top the tomatoes with the cheese and cook until it has melted slightly.

❷ PREPARE THE EGGS

While the tomatoes and cheese are cooking, place the eggs and dill in a large bowl. Season to taste and beat until well combined. Pour the egg mixture over the tomatoes and melted cheese and increase the heat to medium. Cover partially and cook until the top is beginning to set.

❸ FLIP AND FINISH

Place a large plate over the pan and flip it over to transfer the frittata. Reduce the heat to low and return the frittata to the pan, uncooked side up. Cook for another 2–3 minutes, or until the underneath is golden brown and set. Remove from the heat. Slice the frittata into wedges, and serve immediately.

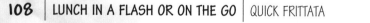

PLAN OF ACTION! ❶ COOK TOMATOES → ❷ PREPARE EGGS → ❸ FLIP AND FINISH

FAVA BEAN TORTILLA

This Spanish recipe combines eggs with lightly cooked fava beans—instead of the usual potatoes—for a flavorful yet quick lunch. You could even cut it into bite-sized pieces to serve as tapas.

SERVES 4–6 • **READY IN** 20 mins

INGREDIENTS

- 4 tbsp olive oil
- 1lb 2oz (500g) fava beans, shelled
- 2 tbsp white wine or dry sherry
- 4 large eggs
- 1 tsp fresh marjoram leaves
- salt and freshly ground black pepper

1 COOK THE BEANS

Heat 1 tablespoon of the oil in a small frying pan. Remove any wrinkled skins from the beans, add them to the pan, and cook for 1 minute, turning them over once. Then add the wine, stir to mix, and cook until the alcohol evaporates. Reduce the heat to a simmer, cover, and cook for 5–6 minutes or until the beans are just soft and the liquid has almost evaporated. Remove from the heat and let cool.

2 PREPARE THE EGGS

Place the eggs and marjoram leaves in a large bowl. Season to taste and beat well to combine. Then add the bean mixture to the bowl and stir well to mix.

3 COOK THE TORTILLA

Heat the remaining oil in the pan. Pour in the egg and bean mixture and spread it out in an even layer. Cook the tortilla over low heat, neatening the edges with a spatula, until the top is beginning to set and the underneath is golden brown.

4 FLIP AND FINISH

Flip the tortilla over (see step 4, opposite) and cook for another 2–3 minutes or until the tortilla is firm but still juicy in the middle. Serve warm or cool.

PLAN OF ACTION! → 1 COOK BEANS → 2 PREPARE EGGS → 3 COOK TORTILLA → 4 FLIP AND FINISH

RECYCLED LEFTOVERS

CHICKEN

Cooked chicken is a great addition to all sorts of meals; simply shred it into small pieces to make it go further before adding to sandwiches, wraps, or salads. Keep cooled cooked chicken, covered, in the fridge for up to 3 days.

CHICKEN TACOS
Toss 3½oz (100g) shredded chicken with a dash of cider vinegar and a pinch each of red pepper flakes and smoked paprika. Layer in taco shells with salsa and guacamole (see p146), and thinly sliced red onions.

OR

CHICKEN SOUP
Cook 1 onion (chopped), ½ stalk celery (chopped), 1 carrot (diced) in butter until they begin to soften. Stir in 1 tbsp all-purpose flour and cook for 2 minutes. Add 2 cups chicken stock and simmer for 10 minutes, until the vegetables are tender. Add 3½oz (100g) cooked, shredded chicken and cook until heated through. Season to taste and serve scattered with chopped parsley.

OR

Barbecue chicken sandwich (p68) • Chicken and apple salad pita pocket (p78) • Shredded chicken in yellow curry sauce pita pocket (p79) • Asian noodle salad (p88) • Spicy Asian chicken salad (p98) • Red curry in a hurry (p134)

BREAD

Tear leftover bread, toast it, and add it to a panzanella. Bread crumbs are also a great staple—they act as a binding agent in meatballs, sausages, and burgers, and make a crispy coating or crust for baked and fried foods.

PANZANELLA
Toss 2 slices of stale bread (cut into bite-sized pieces), 3½oz (100g) ripe tomatoes (chopped), ½ red onion (thinly sliced), and ¼ cucumber (chopped) with 1 tsp red wine vinegar and 3 tsp extra virgin olive oil, and season to taste. Set aside for half an hour, before serving with a small handful each of chopped parsley and torn basil scattered over.

OR

EASY BREAD CRUMBS
Freeze slices of bread and grate using a cheese grater.

OR

For whole pieces or slices:
Strawberry-stuffed French toast (p40) • Sweet potato soup (pp82–3 for the croutons) • The Bruschetta Bar (pp180–1)
For bread crumbs:
Chicken schnitzel (pp118–19) • Classic beef burgers (p121) • Harissa-spiced lamb chops (pp206–7)

Transforming your leftovers into tasty new meals is a quick and easy way to save both time and money on tomorrow's lunch or dinner. It can be a good idea to deliberately cook more of the ingredients below than you need, as these staples are particularly versatile. The quantities below are for 1 serving.

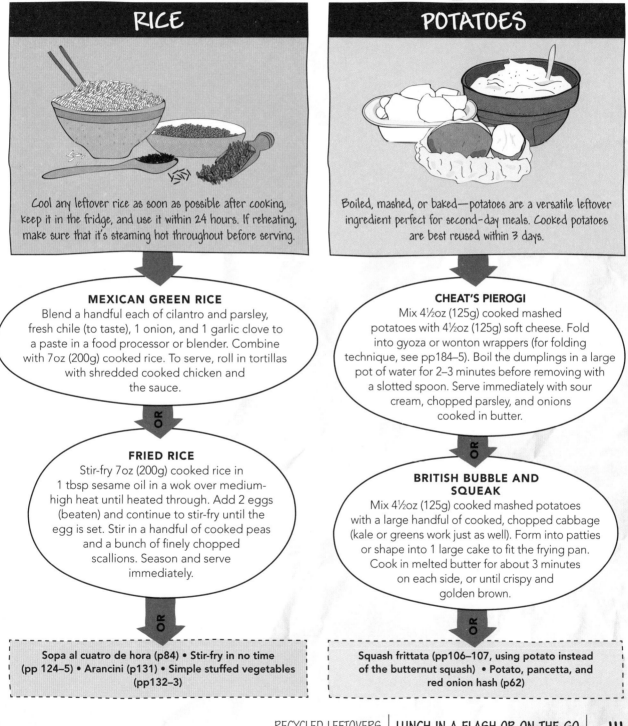

RICE

Cool any leftover rice as soon as possible after cooking, keep it in the fridge, and use it within 24 hours. If reheating, make sure that it's steaming hot throughout before serving.

MEXICAN GREEN RICE
Blend a handful each of cilantro and parsley, fresh chile (to taste), 1 onion, and 1 garlic clove to a paste in a food processor or blender. Combine with 7oz (200g) cooked rice. To serve, roll in tortillas with shredded cooked chicken and the sauce.

OR

FRIED RICE
Stir-fry 7oz (200g) cooked rice in 1 tbsp sesame oil in a wok over medium-high heat until heated through. Add 2 eggs (beaten) and continue to stir-fry until the egg is set. Stir in a handful of cooked peas and a bunch of finely chopped scallions. Season and serve immediately.

OR

Sopa al cuatro de hora (p84) • Stir-fry in no time (pp 124–5) • Arancini (p131) • Simple stuffed vegetables (pp132–3)

POTATOES

Boiled, mashed, or baked—potatoes are a versatile leftover ingredient perfect for second-day meals. Cooked potatoes are best reused within 3 days.

CHEAT'S PIEROGI
Mix 4½oz (125g) cooked mashed potatoes with 4½oz (125g) soft cheese. Fold into gyoza or wonton wrappers (for folding technique, see pp184–5). Boil the dumplings in a large pot of water for 2–3 minutes before removing with a slotted spoon. Serve immediately with sour cream, chopped parsley, and onions cooked in butter.

OR

BRITISH BUBBLE AND SQUEAK
Mix 4½oz (125g) cooked mashed potatoes with a large handful of cooked, chopped cabbage (kale or greens work just as well). Form into patties or shape into 1 large cake to fit the frying pan. Cook in melted butter for about 3 minutes on each side, or until crispy and golden brown.

OR

Squash frittata (pp106–107, using potato instead of the butternut squash) • Potato, pancetta, and red onion hash (p62)

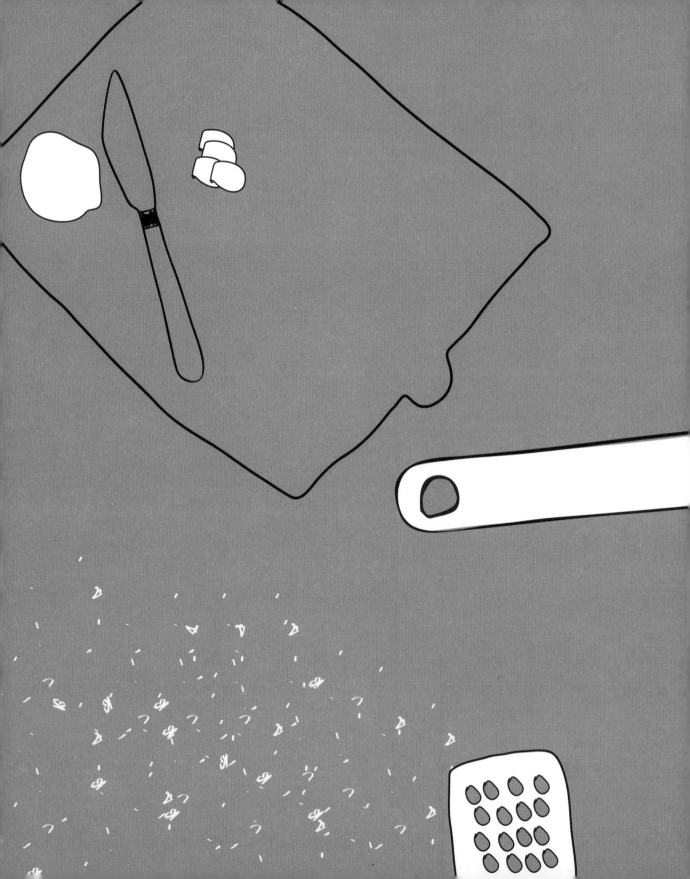

QUICK WEEKNIGHT DINNERS

INGREDIENTS

salt and freshly ground black pepper

1¼lb (550g) new potatoes, well scrubbed and chopped into bite-sized chunks

7oz (200g) hot-smoked mackerel fillets, skinned

2oz (60g) baby salad leaves

2 tbsp chopped dill

2 tbsp chopped chives

7oz (200g) cooked beets (not in vinegar), roughly chopped

baguette, to serve

FOR THE DRESSING
¼ cup extra virgin olive oil
juice of 1 lemon
1 tsp whole-grain mustard
1 tsp honey
1 garlic clove, finely chopped

④
**DRESS
AND SERVE**

HERBED MACKEREL SALAD

Throw together this fragrant salad for a light dinner packed with flavor—and then mop up the delicious dressing with a crispy baguette. Smoked mackerel is great to have in the fridge because it's inexpensive and high in protein.

SERVES 4 • READY IN 20 mins

❶ COOK THE POTATOES

Bring a large pan of salted water to a boil, add the potato chunks, and cook for 10–15 minutes, or until tender. Drain and set aside.

❷ PREPARE THE MACKEREL

Meanwhile, break the mackerel into bite-sized pieces, removing any bones you find as you go, and place in a large serving bowl. Add the salad leaves and herbs and gently toss together.

❸ MAKE THE DRESSING

Place the dressing ingredients in a small bowl, season, and whisk together with a fork.

❹ DRESS, COMBINE, AND SERVE

Add the warm potatoes to the serving bowl, pour in the dressing, and stir gently. Add the beets and serve immediately with the baguette.

TIP – Roll the lemon across the counter before squeezing it. You'll get lots more juice from the fruit without having to work as hard.

CHICKEN SALAD WITH RADICCHIO AND ASPARAGUS

PLAN OF ACTION!

This French *salade tiède* or warm salad, is quick to cook and easy to assemble. Crunchy lettuce and garlicky chicken with a punchy dressing makes for a healthy dinner you can put together in minutes.

SERVES 4 • **READY IN** 15 MINUTES

1 COOK THE CHICKEN

Heat 2 tablespoons of the oil in a large non-stick frying pan over medium-high heat. Add the chicken and garlic and cook, stirring, for 5–7 minutes, or until the chicken is tender and cooked through. Stir in the roasted red bell peppers, and season to taste with salt and pepper.

2 COMBINE WITH THE RADICCHIO

Meanwhile, put the radicchio leaves in a large serving bowl. Remove the chicken from the pan using a slotted spoon and place in the bowl with the radicchio.

3 COOK THE ASPARAGUS

Add the asparagus to the oil remaining in the pan and cook, stirring constantly, for 1–2 minutes, or until just tender. Transfer to the bowl with the chicken.

4 DRESS, TOSS, AND EAT

Whisk together the remaining 2 tablespoons of the oil, the vinegar, and sugar, then pour into the pan and stir over high heat until well combined. Pour this dressing over the salad and toss quickly so that all the ingredients are well mixed and coated with the dressing. Serve immediately.

You can substitute another vinegar for raspberry; try red wine or cider vinegar.

1	2	3	4
COOK CHICKEN	ADD TO RADICCHIO	COOK ASPARAGUS	DRESS AND EAT

INGREDIENTS

4 tbsp extra virgin olive oil

4 chicken breasts, about 5½oz (150g) each, cut into thin strips

1 garlic clove, finely chopped

2oz (60g) roasted red bell peppers, thinly sliced

salt and freshly ground black pepper

1 small head of radicchio, torn into small pieces

9oz (250g) asparagus spears, each trimmed and cut into 3 pieces

2 tbsp raspberry vinegar

½ tsp sugar

CHICKEN SCHNITZEL

This zesty breaded chicken can be ready in no time!
Serve with a green salad and potato wedges or boiled
baby potatoes for a speedy weeknight dinner.

SERVES 2 • **READY IN** 15 mins

- 2 large skinless chicken breast fillets
- 1½ cups fresh bread crumbs
- grated zest of 1 lemon
- salt and freshly ground black pepper
- 1 tbsp all-purpose flour

- 1 egg, lightly beaten
- 1 tbsp olive oil

FOR THE SAUCE
- juice of 1 lemon
- 4–6 fresh sage leaves, finely chopped

PLASTIC WRAP

1 SANDWICH

chicken breasts

PLASTIC WRAP

Flattening meat makes it an even thickness and reduces the cooking time.

2 POUND

FLATTEN THE CHICKEN

ROLLING PIN

Pound until doubled in area and about ½in (1cm) thick.

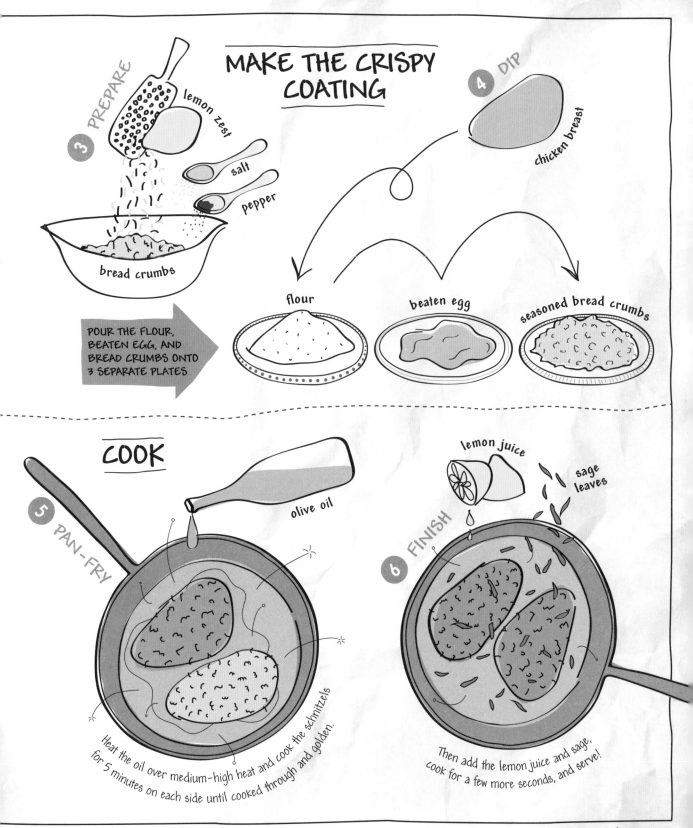

MAKE THE CRISPY COATING

3 PREPARE

lemon zest

salt

pepper

bread crumbs

4 DIP

chicken breast

POUR THE FLOUR, BEATEN EGG, AND BREAD CRUMBS ONTO 3 SEPARATE PLATES

flour

beaten egg

seasoned bread crumbs

COOK

5 PAN-FRY

olive oil

Heat the oil over medium-high heat and cook the schnitzels for 5 minutes on each side until cooked through and golden.

6 FINISH

lemon juice

sage leaves

Then add the lemon juice and sage, cook for a few more seconds, and serve!

CHICKEN CUTLETS WITH LEMON SAUCE

A great time-saving trick for cooking chicken is to pound it to make it thinner; this speeds up the cooking process and makes it more tender. Serve with steamed spring vegetables and new potatoes.

SERVES 4 • **READY IN** 20 mins

INGREDIENTS

- 4 boneless, skinless chicken breasts
- 1 tbsp olive oil
- salt and freshly ground black pepper
- 3 tbsp all-purpose flour
- 1 tbsp butter
- 1 cup chicken stock
- juice of ½ lemon
- 4 heaping tbsp crème fraîche
- 1 tbsp finely chopped thyme leaves
- ½ tsp granulated sugar

❶ FLATTEN THE CHICKEN

Preheat the oven to 300°F (150°C). Pound each chicken breast with the round side of a rolling pin until ½in (1cm) thick all over.

❷ COOK THE CUTLETS

Heat the oil in a large, heavy-bottomed frying pan. Season just 2 tablespoons of the flour with salt and pepper. Dust the chicken with the flour, shaking off any excess. Cook the chicken for 5 minutes on each side over medium heat, until cooked through and golden. Transfer the cooked cutlets to a baking dish and pop in the oven to keep warm.

❸ MAKE THE SAUCE

Wipe the frying pan clean with paper towels. Melt the butter in the pan and scatter over the remaining 1 tablespoon of flour, whisking over medium heat for 1 minute. Gradually add the stock and lemon juice, whisking constantly, and bring to a boil.

❹ THICKEN SAUCE AND SERVE WITH CHICKEN

Add the crème fraîche, thyme, and sugar, and season with salt and pepper to taste. Cook the sauce for 5 minutes, until thick and glossy, whisking constantly with a balloon whisk. Remove the chicken from the oven, spoon out the juices, and add them to the sauce. Slice the chicken on a diagonal and pour the sauce over to serve.

PLAN OF ACTION! ❶ FLATTEN CHICKEN → ❷ COOK CUTLETS → ❸ MAKE SAUCE → ❹ THICKEN SAUCE AND SERVE

CLASSIC BEEF BURGERS

Homemade beef burgers are always worth the effort—they're simple and satisfying to make, and taste so much better than store-bought ones. Serve in a bun with salad and relishes.

MAKES 4 • **READY IN** 20 mins, plus chilling

INGREDIENTS

- 14oz (400g) good-quality ground beef
- ¼ cup fresh white bread crumbs
- 1 egg yolk
- ½ red onion, finely chopped
- ½ tsp dried mustard powder
- ½ tsp celery salt
- 1 tsp Worcestershire sauce
- freshly ground black pepper
- 2 tbsp olive oil

TO SERVE
- 4 burger buns, halved
- 1 head lettuce, shredded
- 2 tomatoes, thickly sliced
- 1 small red onion, finely sliced
- 1 gherkin, finely sliced
- ¼ cup spicy tomato relish

1 PREPARE THE BEEF MIX
In a large bowl, mix together all the burger ingredients (except the oil) until they are well combined.

2 SHAPE THE BURGERS
With damp hands (to help keep the mixture from sticking to your fingers), divide the mixture into 4 balls and roll each one between your palms until smooth. Pressing down with your palms, flatten each ball out into a large, fat disk to a thickness of 1¼in (3cm), and pat the edges in to tidy them up.

3 CHILL THE BURGERS
Place the burgers on a plate, cover with plastic wrap, and chill for 30 minutes (this will help them to keep their shape during cooking).

4 COOK THE BURGERS
Heat the oil in a large frying pan and cook the burgers for 5–6 minutes on each side, until the meat is springy to the touch and the edges are charred.

5 PREPARE THE BUNS AND SERVE
While the burgers are cooking, toast the buns in a dry frying pan over medium heat until golden. Assemble the burgers and buns with a selection of the listed accompaniments, to your liking.

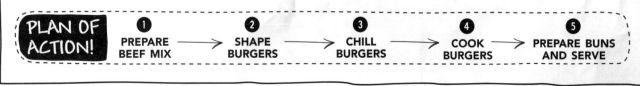

PLAN OF ACTION!
1 PREPARE BEEF MIX → 2 SHAPE BURGERS → 3 CHILL BURGERS → 4 COOK BURGERS → 5 PREPARE BUNS AND SERVE

THAI-SPICED MEATBALLS WITH PEANUT SAUCE

These fragrant, savory bites are perfect with a sweet peanut sauce. Serve them with lime juice squeezed over, and white basmati or jasmine rice on the side, for a filling, Thai-inspired dinner.

SERVES 4 • READY IN 20 mins

INGREDIENTS

FOR THE PEANUT SAUCE

- 1 tbsp vegetable oil
- 1 tsp Thai red curry paste
- 2 tbsp crunchy peanut butter
- 1 tbsp brown sugar
- 1 tbsp lemon juice
- 1 cup coconut milk

FOR THE MEATBALLS

- 1lb (450g) lean ground beef or pork, or a combination of both
- 1 garlic clove, finely chopped
- 1 tsp lemongrass purée
- 1 tbsp chopped cilantro
- 1 tbsp Thai red curry paste
- 1 tbsp lemon juice
- 1 tbsp Thai fish sauce
- 1 egg
- salt and freshly ground black pepper
- rice flour, for dusting
- sunflower oil, for frying
- lime wedges, to garnish

① MAKE THE PEANUT SAUCE

Heat the oil in a small saucepan, add the curry paste, and cook for 1 minute. Gradually stir in the rest of the ingredients, then bring to a boil. Reduce the heat and simmer for 5 minutes, or until thickened. If it is too thick, stir in a little water.

② PREPARE THE MIXTURE

Meanwhile, combine the ground meat, garlic, lemongrass, cilantro, curry paste, lemon juice, Thai fish sauce, and egg, and season to taste with salt and pepper. Roll the mixture into small walnut-sized balls and dust with the rice flour.

③ COOK THE MEATBALLS

Heat the oil in a frying pan. Cook the meatballs in batches until browned and cooked through.

④ DRAIN AND SERVE

Drain on paper towels, then serve hot, with the warm peanut sauce and lime wedges.

PLAN OF ACTION! ① **MAKE PEANUT SAUCE** → ② **PREPARE MIXTURE** → ③ **COOK MEATBALLS** → ④ **DRAIN AND SERVE**

DAN DAN NOODLES

The spicy Szechuan classic, named after the carrying pole used by street vendors selling the dish, has been simplified here to include easily available ingredients. Vary the chile heat levels to your taste.

SERVES 4 • READY IN 20 mins

INGREDIENTS

- 10oz (300g) dried Chinese egg noodles
- salt
- 7oz (200g) small broccoli florets
- ¼ cup soy sauce
- 1 tbsp tahini paste
- 1 tbsp cornstarch
- 2 tsp sesame oil
- 2 tsp chili oil
- 1 tbsp balsamic vinegar
- 1 tsp granulated sugar
- ⅔ cup chicken stock
- 2 tbsp sunflower oil
- 2 garlic cloves, finely chopped
- 1in (3cm) piece of fresh ginger, finely chopped
- 12oz (350g) ground pork
- bunch of scallions, finely chopped, to serve
- 1¾oz (50g) salted peanuts, roughly chopped, to serve (optional)

❶ COOK THE NOODLES AND BROCCOLI

Cook the noodles in a large pan of boiling salted water according to the package instructions. Drain well. Keep them in a bowl of cold water until needed (to prevent them from sticking together). Meanwhile, cook the broccoli for 2 minutes in a pan of boiling salted water, then drain and rinse under cold water. This stops the cooking process and preserves the color of the broccoli, keeping it crisp and bright.

❷ MAKE THE SAUCE

Whisk the soy sauce, tahini, and cornstarch to a thick paste, then whisk in the sesame oil, chili oil, balsamic vinegar, sugar, and stock.

❸ STIR-FRY THE VEGGIES

Heat the sunflower oil in a large wok and stir-fry the garlic and ginger for 1 minute, until it starts to color. Add the pork and stir-fry over high heat, breaking it up with a wooden spoon, until it browns. Add the sauce and allow to boil for about 2 minutes, until it thickens.

❹ ADD THE NOODLES AND SERVE

Add the drained noodles and broccoli, stirring them in well to make sure they are well coated with the sauce and heated through. Serve scattered with the scallions and peanuts (if using).

PLAN OF ACTION! ❶ COOK NOODLES AND BROCCOLI → ❷ MAKE SAUCE → ❸ STIR-FRY VEGGIES → ❹ ADD NOODLES AND SERVE

STIR-FRY IN NO TIME

1 GET SET...

- Grab a wok—the ideal pan for stir-frying. Being thin, it heats up quickly, and its curved shape creates a large surface area for cooking.

- Avoid woks with nonstick coatings, which can prevent the wok from reaching the high temperatures required for stir-frying.

- No wok? No worries—any large deep-sided frying pan will do!

- For stirring, use any heatproof spoon (the longer the handle the better, to keep your hand away from the heat). Be careful not to leave it in the wok unattended, as the heat may cause it to melt or burn.

2 GET PREPPED...

- Prepare all your ingredients before you start—there won't be time later.

- Cut your ingredients into small, similar-sized pieces to allow quick and even cooking.

- Cook your rice or noodles first, then drain and set aside. Add to the wok once the other ingredients are ready.

- Use peanut or sunflower oil for cooking (2 tbsp), as these oils can be heated to very high temperatures without burning.

- Heat the wok before adding the oil (oil will slow the heating process).

- Swirl the oil around the wok and wait until it is smoking hot before adding any ingredients.

3 GO!

- Add chiles and spices first so their flavors can infuse the cooking oil. Then add your ingredients according to how long each takes to cook:

  - Start with proteins, such as meat, fish, or tofu (5½oz/150g). Peanuts or boiled eggs can be added later.

  - Then add hard vegetables, such as carrots or broccoli (2½oz/75g).

  - Now add softer vegetables, such as onion, mushrooms, leafy greens, and peppers (2½oz/75g).

  - Add a pinch or splash (to taste) of seasonings, sauces, and herbs toward the end of cooking.

  - Finally, return the cooked rice or noodles to the wok to heat through (2½oz/75g), dried weight).

KEY STIR-FRY INGREDIENTS

PROTEINS

Beef • Pork • Chicken • Shrimp • Calamari • Salmon • Peanuts • Tofu • Boiled eggs

VEGETABLES

Bean sprouts • Onions • Scallions • Shallots • Garlic • Bamboo shoots • Water chestnuts • Bok choy • Carrots • Green beans • Snow peas • Shiitake mushrooms • Enoki mushrooms • Edamame beans • Oyster mushrooms • Daikon radish • Cabbage • Napa cabbage • Soy bean sprouts

Stir-frying is the ultimate in quick cooking. Make sure your stir-fries are always spot on by following our three steps to success. Then, find out how to give your key stir-fry ingredients a cuisine-based makeover with a few traditional flavorings. The suggested quantities serve 1.

STIR-FRY FLAVORS

KOREAN-STYLE

FLAVORS Red bell pepper • Chile powder • Red chile paste • Korean soybean paste • Korean soy sauce • Sesame oil • Apricot syrup • Sake or mirin

TYPICAL INGREDIENTS Tofu • Napa cabbage • Soy bean sprouts • Daikon radish

VIETNAMESE-STYLE

FLAVORS Cloves • Cinnamon stick • Star anise • Fish sauce • Lemongrass • Shrimp paste

TYPICAL INGREDIENTS Beef • Pork • Shrimp • Calamari • Rice vermicelli • Flat rice noodles • Sticky rice • Oyster mushrooms • Pickled bamboo

JAPANESE-STYLE

FLAVORS Shoyu or tamari • Mirin • Rice vinegar • Teriyaki sauce • Sake • Pickled ginger (*gari*)

TYPICAL INGREDIENTS Tofu • Eggs • Salmon • Shiitake mushrooms • Enoki mushrooms • Cabbage • Edamame beans • Daikon radish • Sticky rice • Soba noodles • Udon noodles • Mizuna (as a garnish)

INDONESIAN-STYLE

FLAVORS Galangal • Shrimp paste • Palm sugar • Lime juice • Turmeric • Nutmeg • *Kecap manis* (a sweet, syrup-like soy sauce)

TYPICAL INGREDIENTS Eggs • Peanuts • Beef • Pork • Green beans • Scallions • Snow peas • Shallots • Long-grain rice • Wheat noodles (*bami*) • Rice vermicelli (*bihun*) • Flat rice noodles (*bun*)

THAI-STYLE

FLAVORS Tamarind paste • Thai sweet basil • Lemongrass • *Nam pla* (fish sauce) • Thai shrimp paste • Lime juice

TYPICAL INGREDIENTS Shrimp • Chicken • Peanuts • Eggs • Bean sprouts • Scallions • Jasmine rice • Flat rice noodles • Rice vermicelli

SZECHUAN-STYLE

FLAVORS Szechuan peppercorns • Sesame paste • Ginger • Star anise • Cinnamon • Garlic

TYPICAL INGREDIENTS Peanuts • Egg noodles

RICE AND NOODLES

Sticky rice • Soba noodles • Udon noodles • Egg noodles • Short-grain white rice • Long-grain white rice • Jasmine rice • Flat rice noodles • Rice vermicelli • Wheat noodles

THAI-STYLE STIR-FRIED BEEF IN LETTUCE CUPS

This is a fun way to serve and eat stir-fry—in individual baby gem lettuce cups! You can dive into this as it is, eating the lettuce cups with your hands, or serve with basmati rice or quinoa for a more substantial meal.

SERVES 4–6 • READY IN 15 mins

1 BLANCH THE BROCCOLI

Bring a large pan of salted water to a boil and blanch the broccoli for 1 minute, then drain and rinse it under cold water. Set aside.

2 STIR-FRY THE FRESH INGREDIENTS

Heat the sunflower oil in a wok or a large, deep-sided frying pan. Add the scallions, garlic, ginger, carrot, cilantro stalks, and chile and cook for a couple of minutes until colored slightly.

3 ADD THE BEEF

Add the ground beef and continue to cook over high heat until the meat is well browned.

4 COMBINE, FLAVOR, AND SERVE

Return the broccoli to the pan and add the fish sauce, soy sauce, lime juice, and sugar. Mix well, cooking for a minute or two until the broccoli is piping hot. Stir in the cilantro leaves and divide between individual "cups" of baby gem lettuce.

Why not try substituting ground turkey, ground pork, tofu, or shrimp for the beef?

1 BLANCH BROCCOLI → **2** STIR-FRY INGREDIENTS → **3** ADD BEEF → **4** COMBINE AND SERVE

INGREDIENTS

salt

3½oz (100g) broccoli florets, cut very small

2 tbsp sunflower oil

bunch of scallions, finely chopped

2 garlic cloves, crushed

1in (3cm) fresh ginger, finely chopped

1 large carrot, cut into strips

1 tbsp finely chopped cilantro stalks, plus a handful of cilantro leaves, roughly chopped

1 red chile, seeded and finely chopped

14oz (400g) ground beef

1 tbsp fish sauce

2 tbsp soy sauce

1 tbsp lime juice

1 tsp superfine sugar

baby gem lettuce leaves, to serve

INGREDIENTS

10oz (300g) medium or thick dried rice noodles

2 tbsp sunflower oil

2 eggs, lightly beaten

1 tsp shrimp paste (optional)

2 hot red chiles, seeded and finely chopped

3 boneless, skinless chicken breasts, cut into ¼in (5mm) slices

bunch of scallions, finely chopped

splash of Thai fish sauce, such as *nam pla*

juice of 1 lime

1 tbsp brown sugar

salt and freshly ground black pepper

5½oz (150g) unsalted peanuts, toasted in a dry wok or frying pan

handful of cilantro leaves, finely chopped

lime wedges, to serve

PLAN OF ACTION!

1. SOAK NOODLES →
2. COOK EGG →
3. STIR-FRY CHICKEN →
4. ADD FLAVORINGS

PAD THAI

Originating from roadside food stands in Thailand, this zingy noodle dish is designed to be quick to cook and easy to assemble—ideal for the time-limited chef! Experiment with different kinds of rice noodles to find your favorite.

SERVES 4 • **READY IN** 20 mins

❶ SOAK THE NOODLES

Put the noodles in a large bowl, cover with boiling water, and leave for 8 minutes, or until soft. Drain and set aside.

❷ COOK THE EGG

Meanwhile, put 1 tablespoon of the oil in a large wok over high heat and swirl around the pan. Add the beaten egg and swirl it around the wok for about a minute, or until it begins to set—don't let it set completely—then remove, chop, and set aside.

❸ STIR-FRY THE CHICKEN

Add the remaining 2 tablespoons of oil to the pan, then add the shrimp paste (if using) and chiles and stir. With the heat still high, add the chicken and stir vigorously for 5 minutes, or until no longer pink.

❹ ADD FLAVORINGS

Stir in the scallions, fish sauce, lime juice, and sugar and toss together well. Cook for a few minutes until the sugar has dissolved, then season well with salt and pepper. Return the egg to the pan.

❺ COMBINE WITH THE NOODLES

Add the noodles to the pan and toss together to coat with the sauce, then add half the peanuts and half the cilantro and toss again. Transfer to a large, shallow warmed serving bowl and scatter with the rest of the peanuts and cilantro. Garnish with lime wedges to serve.

For a vegetarian option, omit the chicken, shrimp paste, and fish sauce and substitute fried tofu that's been marinated in soy sauce, crushed garlic, lime juice, and chile.

OVEN-BAKED RISOTTO

This risotto needs much less of your time than the traditional method—instead of constantly stirring for 20 minutes, you cook everything briefly before popping it in the oven to do its thing!

SERVES 4 • **READY IN** 20–30 mins
SPECIAL EQUIPMENT Large, heavy-bottomed heatproof casserole

INGREDIENTS

- 2 tbsp butter
- 1 tbsp olive oil
- 1 onion, finely chopped
- 2 garlic cloves, finely chopped
- 10oz (300g) mixed mushrooms, such as crimini, shiitake, and oyster, roughly chopped
- 14oz (400g) risotto rice
- 2½ cups vegetable or chicken stock
- ⅔ cup dry white wine
- salt and freshly ground black pepper
- 10oz (300g) cooked chicken, chopped into bite-sized pieces
- 1¼oz (40g) grated Grana Padano cheese, plus extra to serve
- ¼ cup chopped parsley leaves

1 COOK THE ONION AND GARLIC

Preheat the oven to 400°F (200°C). Heat the butter and oil in a large, heavy-bottomed heatproof casserole over low heat. Once the butter has melted, add the onion and garlic, and cook gently for 3–4 minutes.

2 ADD THE MUSHROOMS, RICE, AND STOCK

Add the mushrooms and rice and stir well to coat in the butter and oil. Pour in the stock and wine, bring to a boil, season, and stir well.

3 COVER AND BAKE

Cover and cook in the oven for 15 minutes or until the rice is tender, stirring a couple of times.

4 ADD THE CHICKEN AND CHEESE

Remove from the oven and stir in the chicken, Grana Padano cheese, and parsley. Return to the oven for 2–3 minutes, or until the chicken is heated through. Serve with pepper and extra Grana Padano, for sprinkling.

For a spinach and hot-smoked salmon risotto, omit the mushrooms and chicken, and stir in 10oz (300g) flaked, hot-smoked almon fillets and 3½oz (100g) spinach 5 minutes before the end of the cooking time.

PLAN OF ACTION!

1 COOK ONION AND GARLIC → 2 ADD MUSHROOMS, RICE, AND STOCK → 3 COVER AND BAKE → 4 ADD CHICKEN AND CHEESE

ARANCINI

A fantastic way to use up leftover risotto, these Italian stuffed rice balls make a light and tasty dinner. Serve alongside a fresh green salad and, if you wish, a spicy tomato sauce.

MAKES 12 • **READY IN** 20 mins, plus resting

INGREDIENTS

- 14oz (400g) cooked, cold risotto
- 2oz (60g) mozzarella cheese, cut into 12 x ½in (1cm) cubes
- ¼ cup all-purpose flour
- 1 egg, beaten
- 1 cup day-old bread crumbs or Japanese panko bread crumbs
- 3½ cups sunflower oil, for deep-frying

❶ MOLD THE RISOTTO BALLS

Keep your hands damp to mold the risotto balls. Take a walnut-sized spoonful of the risotto rice and mold it, in your palm, so it creates a flattened circle. Place a cube of the mozzarella in the middle of the rice and mold the rice around it, rolling it to make a ball. Make sure that the mozzarella is well covered, and take care to pack the risotto tightly around. Continue until you have 12 balls.

❷ ROLL IN BREAD CRUMBS

Put the flour, egg, and bread crumbs separately in 3 wide, shallow bowls. Roll each risotto ball first in the flour, then in the egg, and finally coat it well in the bread crumbs. Place on a plate, cover with plastic wrap, and rest in the fridge for at least 30 minutes (this will help the coating to stick).

❸ HEAT THE OIL

Heat the oil in a large, heavy-bottomed saucepan to a depth of 4in (10cm). It will be ready when a small piece of bread dropped in sizzles and turns golden brown.

❹ FRY THE ARANCINI

Fry the risotto balls a few at a time, for two minutes, until golden brown all over. Remove with a slotted spoon and drain on paper towels. Keep warm in the oven while you cook the rest.

TIP – You can make arancini with all sorts of risottos, but ensure that the kind you use is fairly smooth in texture, as then the mixture will adhere more easily to the bread crumb coating. If you're making these with leftover Oven-Baked Risotto (see opposite), ensure that the mushrooms are chopped up into small pieces.

PLAN OF ACTION! ❶ MOLD RISOTTO BALLS → ❷ ROLL IN BREAD CRUMBS → ❸ HEAT OIL → ❹ FRY ARANCINI

SIMPLE STUFFED VEGETABLES

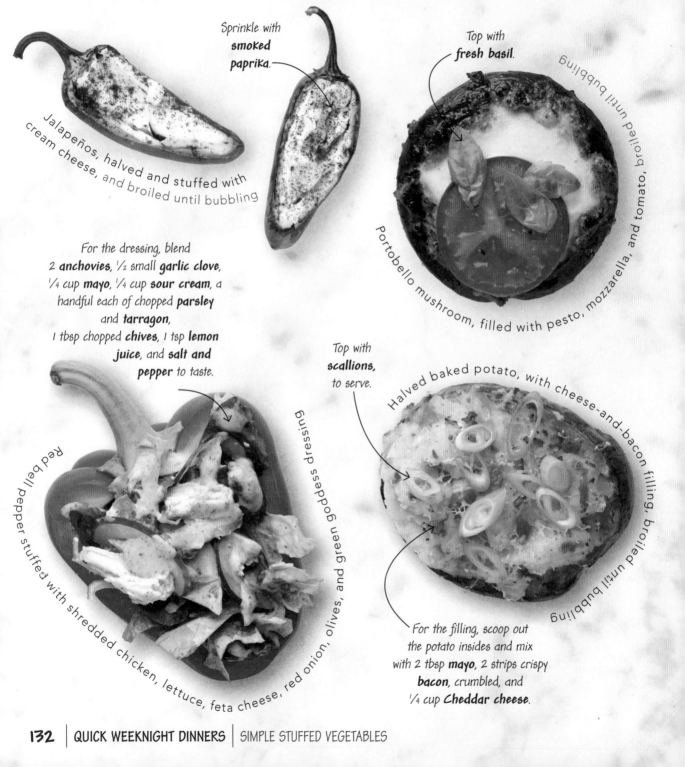

Sprinkle with **smoked paprika**.

Jalapeños, halved and stuffed with cream cheese, and broiled until bubbling

Top with **fresh basil**.

Portobello mushroom, filled with pesto, mozzarella, and tomato, broiled until bubbling

For the dressing, blend 2 **anchovies**, ½ small **garlic clove**, ¼ cup **mayo**, ¼ cup **sour cream**, a handful each of chopped **parsley** and **tarragon**, 1 tbsp chopped **chives**, 1 tsp **lemon juice**, and **salt and pepper** to taste.

Top with **scallions**, to serve.

Halved baked potato, with cheese-and-bacon filling, broiled until bubbling

Red bell pepper stuffed with shredded chicken, lettuce, feta cheese, red onion, olives, and green goddess dressing

For the filling, scoop out the potato insides and mix with 2 tbsp **mayo**, 2 strips crispy **bacon**, crumbled, and ¼ cup **Cheddar cheese**.

These delightful stuffed vegetables are as delicious as they are eye-catching. They're easy to prepare for comforting, everyday dinners and look great for when you're entertaining friends. Instead of these fillings, you could use mashed sweet potato or corn, seasoned bread crumbs, rice, or quinoa.

Halved and slightly hollowed out avocado with an egg cracked in, topped with cayenne pepper and sea salt

Bake at 425°F (220°C) until the egg is set.

Drizzle with **olive oil** and broil until bubbling.

Tomato stuffed with cooked couscous, fresh basil and oregano, and topped with Parmesan

Halved eggplant stuffed with roughly chopped chorizo, onion, and red and green bell peppers

Top with **ricotta cheese** and bake at 350°F (180°C) until golden.

ONE-POT MEALS

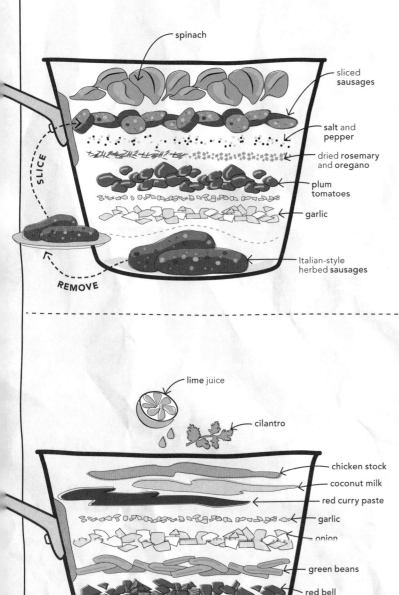

spinach

sliced sausages

salt and pepper

dried **rosemary** and oregano

plum tomatoes

garlic

Italian-style herbed **sausages**

SLICE

REMOVE

lime juice

cilantro

chicken stock

coconut milk

red curry paste

garlic

onion

green beans

red bell pepper

chicken breast

MEDITERRANEAN MIX

1 Heat 1 tbsp **olive oil** over medium heat.

2 Add 7oz (200g) good quality Italian-style herbed **sausages** and cook for 3 minutes on each side, or until browned and cooked through. Remove the sausages and set aside.

3 Stir in 1 chopped onion, 2 finely chopped **garlic** cloves, and 14oz (400g) chopped fresh **plum tomatoes**, along with 1 tbsp dried **oregano**, 1 tbsp dried **rosemary**, **salt**, and **pepper**. Cook for 5 minutes.

4 Return the sausages, sliced, to the pan, and add 2 big handfuls of fresh **spinach**. Stir together to wilt the spinach. Serve with **crusty bread**.

RED CURRY IN A HURRY

1 Heat 1 tbsp **coconut oil** over medium heat.

2 Add 1 **chicken breast**, cut into strips, and cook until the meat is cooked through.

3 Place 14oz (400g) chopped **red bell peppers**, 10oz (300g) sliced **green beans**, 1 chopped **onion**, and 2 finely sliced cloves of **garlic** into the pan. Stir to coat.

4 Stir in 2 tbsp **red curry paste**, 1¼ cups **coconut milk**, and ¼ cup **chicken stock**. Bring to a rapid simmer and cook for 10–12 minutes, stirring frequently.

5 Add a squeeze of fresh **lime** juice, garnish with **cilantro**, and serve with cooked **basmati rice**.

What could be simpler and quicker than cooking a whole meal in just one pot or pan? With these recipes you can have a satisfying dinner for two on the table in 20 minutes, and only one pot to clean up! All you need is a large skillet or deep-sided frying pan and a few simple ingredients.

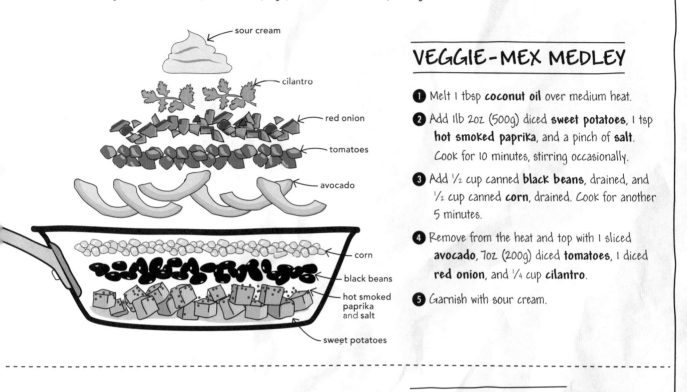

VEGGIE-MEX MEDLEY

1. Melt 1 tbsp **coconut oil** over medium heat.

2. Add 1lb 2oz (500g) diced **sweet potatoes**, 1 tsp **hot smoked paprika**, and a pinch of **salt**. Cook for 10 minutes, stirring occasionally.

3. Add ½ cup canned **black beans**, drained, and ½ cup canned **corn**, drained. Cook for another 5 minutes.

4. Remove from the heat and top with 1 sliced **avocado**, 7oz (200g) diced **tomatoes**, 1 diced **red onion**, and ¼ cup **cilantro**.

5. Garnish with sour cream.

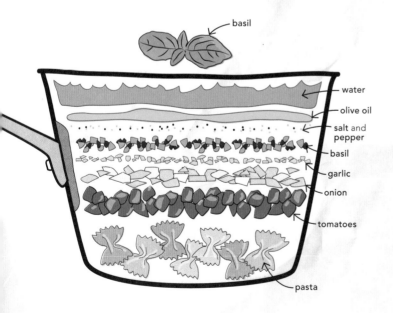

ONE-POT PASTA

1. Add 12oz (350g) **pasta**, such as farfalle, 7oz (200g) chopped fresh **tomatoes**, 1 chopped **onion**, 4 finely chopped **garlic** cloves, a large handful of torn **basil**, **salt**, **pepper**, ¼ cup **olive oil**, and 4 cups **water**.

2. Bring to a boil over high heat and simmer.

3. Garnish with fresh basil and serve.

PESTO, PRONTO!

This versatile Italian sauce can be tossed with cooked pasta, spread on crostini, beaten with crème fraîche for a dip, or even used on tarts or pizza. Blend the ingredients in a food processor or mortar and pestle, then adjust to taste. Each recipe makes 1 jar (10oz/ 300g), which will keep in the fridge for up to 1 week.

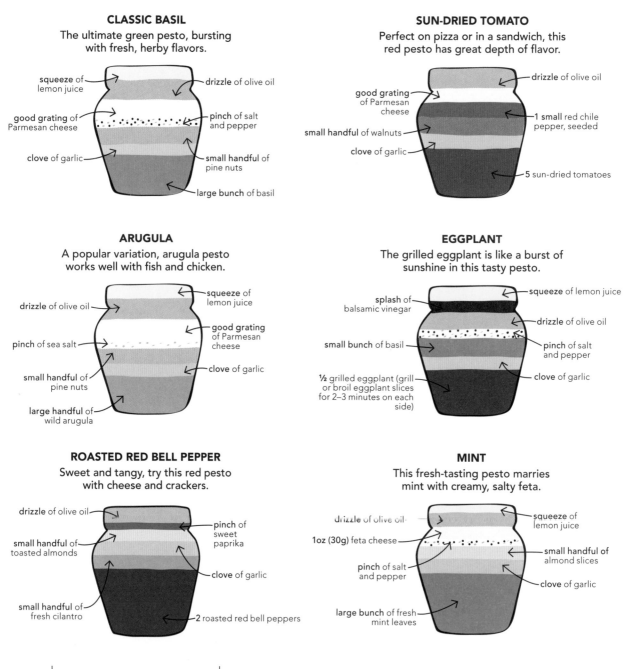

CLASSIC BASIL
The ultimate green pesto, bursting with fresh, herby flavors.

squeeze of lemon juice
drizzle of olive oil
good grating of Parmesan cheese
pinch of salt and pepper
clove of garlic
small handful of pine nuts
large bunch of basil

SUN-DRIED TOMATO
Perfect on pizza or in a sandwich, this red pesto has great depth of flavor.

drizzle of olive oil
good grating of Parmesan cheese
small handful of walnuts
clove of garlic
1 small red chile pepper, seeded
5 sun-dried tomatoes

ARUGULA
A popular variation, arugula pesto works well with fish and chicken.

squeeze of lemon juice
drizzle of olive oil
good grating of Parmesan cheese
pinch of sea salt
clove of garlic
small handful of pine nuts
large handful of wild arugula

EGGPLANT
The grilled eggplant is like a burst of sunshine in this tasty pesto.

splash of balsamic vinegar
squeeze of lemon juice
drizzle of olive oil
small bunch of basil
pinch of salt and pepper
clove of garlic
½ grilled eggplant (grill or broil eggplant slices for 2–3 minutes on each side)

ROASTED RED BELL PEPPER
Sweet and tangy, try this red pesto with cheese and crackers.

drizzle of olive oil
pinch of sweet paprika
small handful of toasted almonds
clove of garlic
small handful of fresh cilantro
2 roasted red bell peppers

MINT
This fresh-tasting pesto marries mint with creamy, salty feta.

drizzle of olive oil
squeeze of lemon juice
1oz (30g) feta cheese
small handful of almond slices
pinch of salt and pepper
clove of garlic
large bunch of fresh mint leaves

BROCCOLI AND BLUE CHEESE PASTA SAUCE

Stir this delicious sauce though any pasta for a simple and quick dinner. For four people, cook about 14oz (400g) of dried pasta according to the package instructions.

SERVES 4 • **READY IN** 20 mins

SPECIAL EQUIPMENT Food processor

INGREDIENTS

- 9oz (250g) broccoli, cut into bite-sized florets
- ¾ cup low-fat crème fraîche
- 7oz (200g) Dolcelatte or Gorgonzola cheese, rind removed and roughly chopped
- finely grated zest of 1 lemon, plus 1 tbsp lemon juice
- ¼ tsp ground nutmeg
- freshly ground black pepper
- 3 tbsp chopped walnuts, to serve

1 PREPARE THE BROCCOLI PURÉE

Place the broccoli in a steamer and steam for about 5 minutes or until just tender. Drain well and transfer to a food processor. Process to a smooth purée.

2 MAKE THE SAUCE

While the broccoli is steaming, make the sauce. Place the crème fraîche and cheese in a saucepan. Cook over low heat, stirring constantly, until well combined and smooth. Then stir in the lemon zest, lemon juice, and nutmeg. Season with a good grinding of pepper and stir well.

3 COMBINE AND SERVE

Add the broccoli purée to the cheese mixture and stir well to combine. To serve, pour the sauce over cooked pasta, mix to coat, and sprinkle with the walnuts.

> For a **milder** sauce, try replacing the blue cheese with cream cheese and a handful of grated Parmesan.

PLAN OF ACTION!

1 PREPARE BROCCOLI → 2 MAKE SAUCE → 3 COMBINE AND SERVE

SHRIMP AND GARLIC "PASTA"

Also known as "zoodles" (zucchini noodles) the spaghetti-like ribbons of zucchini in this quick and enticing dish offer a healthy, carb- and gluten-free alternative to pasta.

SERVES 4 • **READY IN** 20 mins
SPECIAL EQUIPMENT Julienne peeler

INGREDIENTS

- 6 zucchini
- 1 tbsp olive oil, plus 1 extra
- 1 garlic clove, crushed
- 12 raw shrimp, peeled and deveined
- salt and freshly ground black pepper
- squeeze of lemon juice

1 MAKE THE "PASTA"

Cut off a thin slice along the length of each zucchini (this keeps them from rolling around) and place on a cutting board. Use a julienne peeler to slice the zucchini into thin ribbons, stopping and rotating each zucchini when you reach the seeds.

2 SAUTÉ THE SHRIMP

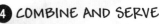

Heat the oil in a large frying pan. Add the garlic and shrimp and sauté until the shrimp are pink and cooked through. Remove from the heat.

3 BLANCH THE "PASTA"

While the shrimp is cooking, blanch (briefly boil) the zucchini. Place enough water to cover the zucchini in a large saucepan. Add a pinch of salt and bring to a boil. Then add the zucchini, cook for 1 minute, and remove. Plunge the zucchini into a bowl of ice water to stop the cooking process. Drain well.

4 COMBINE AND SERVE

Drain the zucchini and place on a serving dish. Drizzle with 1 tablespoon of oil, season to taste, and add a squeeze of lemon juice. Toss to mix, top with the shrimp, and serve.

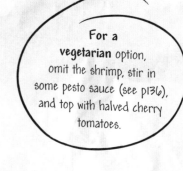

For a **vegetarian** option, omit the shrimp, stir in some pesto sauce (see p136), and top with halved cherry tomatoes.

PLAN OF ACTION!

1 MAKE "PASTA" → **2** SAUTÉ SHRIMP → **3** BLANCH "PASTA" → **4** COMBINE AND SERVE

PEA AND PANCETTA PASTA

This meal can be on the table in just 15 minutes! It's a speedy pasta dish that relies on a handful of pantry essentials to make a satisfying dinner. If you use shell pasta, such as conchigliette, the peas and pieces of pancetta nestle neatly inside.

SERVES 4 • **READY IN** 15 mins

❶ COOK THE PASTA AND PEAS

Cook the pasta in boiling salted water according to the package instructions. A minute or two before the end of cooking, throw the peas in with the pasta to cook through. Drain (reserving a ladleful of the cooking water) and return it to the pan with the reserved water.

❷ COOK THE PANCETTA

Meanwhile, heat the oil in a large frying pan. Cook the pancetta for 3–5 minutes over medium heat until crispy. Add the butter and garlic and cook for another minute, then remove from the heat.

❸ TOSS TOGETHER AND SEASON

Toss the garlicky pancetta through the pasta and peas and follow with the Parmesan cheese. Season well to taste and serve with extra Parmesan cheese.

TIP – There's no need to peel the garlic, just pop a clove into the garlic press with its skin on.

You can use chopped-up bacon if you don't have any pancetta. Choose smoked, thick-cut bacon, as it is most like pancetta in flavor.

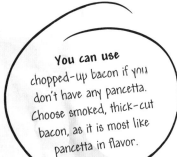

PLAN OF ACTION!

1 COOK PASTA → 2 COOK PANCETTA → 3 TOSS TOGETHER

INGREDIENTS

10oz (300g) dried shell pasta, such as conchigliette

salt and freshly ground black pepper

5½oz (150g) frozen peas or petits pois

2 tbsp olive oil

7oz (200g) pancetta, chopped

2 tbsp butter

2 garlic cloves, crushed

1¾oz (50g) finely grated Parmesan

CHICKEN FAJITAS

These Mexican-style wraps are quick to prepare and fun to assemble. They are traditionally made with chicken or beef, but see pp144–7 for lots more ideas for fillings.

SERVES 4 • READY IN 20 mins

FOR THE MARINADE
- 2 tbsp olive oil
- juice of 1 lime
- 2 tsp ground cumin
- 1 tsp smoked paprika
- 1 tsp dried oregano
- 1 tsp cayenne pepper or chile powder
- salt and freshly ground black pepper

FOR THE FAJITAS
- 2 large boneless, skinless chicken breasts, sliced
- 2 tbsp sunflower oil

- 1 red onion, seeded and cut into ½in (1cm) slices
- 1 red bell pepper, seeded and cut into ½in (1cm) slices
- 8 tortillas

FOR THE SALSA
- 4 large ripe tomatoes
- 1 green chile
- ½ red onion
- handful of cilantro
- juice of 1 lime
- drizzle of olive oil

MAKE THE CHICKEN MIX

1 SLICE chicken breasts

2 SLICE red onion, red bell pepper

3 MIX THEN MARINATE — Combine the sliced chicken, onion, and red bell pepper with the marinade ingredients.

olive oil · lime · cumin · smoked paprika · oregano · cayenne pepper or chile powder · salt · pepper

Chop your fajita ingredients into pieces of the same size for even cooking.

WHILE THE MIX IS MARINATING, MAKE THE SALSA.

MAKE THE SALSA

4 CHOP

tomatoes

red onion

green chile

cilantro

Chop the salsa ingredients into same-sized pieces.

5 MIX

olive oil

lime

pepper

Combine all the salsa ingredients.

COOK THE CHICKEN MIX AND WARM THE TORTILLA

LARGE FRYING PAN

6 COOK

Heat the oil and cook the chicken mix over high heat for 5–7 minutes until tender. Spoon into a serving dish and keep warm.

7 WARM

tortilla

Wipe the frying pan clean with paper towels and warm the tortillas, one at a time, over medium heat.

BUILD THE FAJITA

8 LAYER

salsa

cooked chicken mix

tortilla

FOLDING YOUR FAJITA

1. Place the filling on the tortilla, leaving the bottom quarter empty.

2. Fold up the tortilla from the bottom edge.

3. Fold one side over...

4. ... then fold the other side over.

FAJITA FILLINGS

Tuna and mayo with corn and salad leaves

Warm the **sardines** over low heat.

Canned sardines in tomato sauce with mixed salad leaves

Smoked salmon, cream cheese, and grilled zucchini

Drizzle of **balsamic** vinegar.

Grated Cheddar cheese, cherry tomatoes, cucumber, and mayo

Fajitas, or Mexican-style wraps, are such a versatile choice. It's so easy to replace traditional chicken fillings (see pp142–43) with appetizing meat, fish, or veggie alternatives—either cooked fresh or using up leftovers. Here are some fabulous fillings to try.

Cream cheese, roasted sweet potato, raw spinach leaves, and red pepper flakes

Leftover chilli con carne with arugula leaves, sour cream, and paprika

Cooked shrimp and thousand island dressing with salad

Drizzle with extra virgin **olive oil**.

Hummus and roasted carrots with sunflower seeds and arugula leaves

SPEEDY SALSAS

Why not transform your meal into a Mexican-style feast by adding one of these sensational salsas to your plate? They're also great for serving with tortilla chips or nachos when you've got friends over. Simply dice each ingredient into small, same-sized pieces, mix it all up, then adjust to taste and eat as soon as possible!

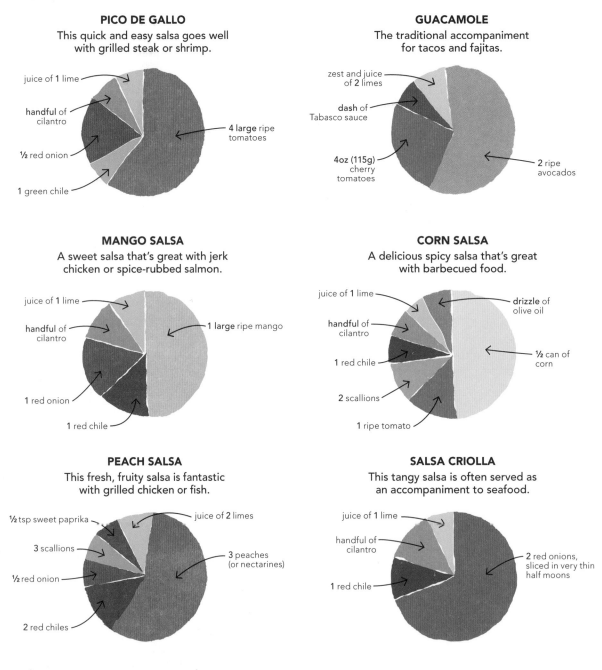

PICO DE GALLO
This quick and easy salsa goes well with grilled steak or shrimp.

- juice of **1** lime
- **handful** of cilantro
- **½** red onion
- **1** green chile
- **4 large** ripe tomatoes

GUACAMOLE
The traditional accompaniment for tacos and fajitas.

- zest and juice of **2** limes
- **dash** of Tabasco sauce
- **4oz (115g)** cherry tomatoes
- **2** ripe avocados

MANGO SALSA
A sweet salsa that's great with jerk chicken or spice-rubbed salmon.

- juice of **1** lime
- **handful** of cilantro
- **1** red onion
- **1** red chile
- **1 large** ripe mango

CORN SALSA
A delicious spicy salsa that's great with barbecued food.

- juice of **1** lime
- **handful** of cilantro
- **1** red chile
- **2** scallions
- **1** ripe tomato
- **drizzle** of olive oil
- **½** can of corn

PEACH SALSA
This fresh, fruity salsa is fantastic with grilled chicken or fish.

- **½** tsp sweet paprika
- **3** scallions
- **½** red onion
- **2** red chiles
- juice of **2** limes
- **3** peaches (or nectarines)

SALSA CRIOLLA
This tangy salsa is often served as an accompaniment to seafood.

- juice of **1** lime
- **handful** of cilantro
- **1** red chile
- **2** red onions, sliced in very thin half moons

BLACK-EYED PEA, SPINACH, AND TOMATO CURRY

A delicious and nutritious meal, this curry makes for a satisfying weeknight dinner that's quicker and cheaper than ordering takeout. Yogurt adds creaminess to the sauce—just be careful not to overcook it, as it will separate.

SERVES 4 • READY IN 20 mins

- -

1 SOFTEN THE ONION

Heat the oil in a large saucepan and add the mustard seeds. When they start to pop, add the garlic, curry leaves, and onion. Cook over medium heat for 5 minutes, or until the onion is soft.

2 COOK THE TOMATO AND SPINACH

Add the green chiles, chile powder, coriander, and turmeric. Mix well and add the tomato pieces. Stir, then add the spinach. Cook over low heat for 5 minutes.

3 ADD THE PEAS AND SERVE

Finally, add the black-eyed peas and salt to taste. Cook for another minute, or until everything is hot. Remove the pan from the heat and slowly add the yogurt, stirring well. Serve warm with naan bread or rice.

TIP – When yogurt is heated too much it separates into solid and liquid layers (curds and whey). Adding the yogurt gradually as the dish cools will ensure that it retains its creaminess.

INGREDIENTS

3 tbsp sunflower oil

½ tsp mustard seeds

2 garlic cloves, finely chopped

10 curry leaves

1 large onion, chopped

2 green chiles, split lengthwise and seeded

½ tsp chile powder

1 tsp ground coriander

½ tsp ground turmeric

3 tomatoes, chopped

3½oz (100g) spinach, chopped

14oz can black-eyed peas, rinsed and drained

salt

1¼ cups plain yogurt

naan bread or rice, to serve

HEART OF PALM AND CRAYFISH GREEN CURRY

Hearts of palm—the edible centers of young palm shoots—have a crunch that offers a textural contrast to the creamy spicy sauce. For added color, why not throw in some cherry tomatoes at step 2?

SERVES 4 • **READY IN** 20 mins

INGREDIENTS

- 5 tbsp coconut cream
- ¼ cup Thai green curry paste
- 1 x 14oz (400g) can hearts of palm, drained and cut into bite-sized pieces
- 4–5 baby corn, each cut in half lengthwise
- light soy sauce, to taste
- 1 x 14oz (400ml) can coconut milk
- 5½oz (150g) cooked crayfish tails
- a few pea eggplants (optional)
- 3 kaffir lime leaves, torn
- 3 green chiles, seeded and thinly sliced at an angle
- handful of Thai (or ordinary) basil leaves, torn
- jasmine rice, to serve

① HEAT THE PASTE, HEARTS OF PALM, AND CORN

Heat the coconut cream in a saucepan, add the curry paste, and cook over high heat for 3 minutes, stirring regularly. Add the hearts of palm and corn and cook for another 3 minutes or until the paste looks scrambled and smells cooked. Season with soy sauce.

② SIMMER THE REMAINING INGREDIENTS AND SERVE

Pour in the coconut milk, stirring gently. Bring to a boil and add the remaining ingredients except the basil. Check the seasoning and adjust if necessary. Simmer for 2 minutes, then stir in the basil. Spoon over jasmine rice in bowls and serve.

If you can't find heart of palm, try green bell pepper, asparagus, or cooked new potatoes instead.

PLAN OF ACTION!

① HEAT PASTE, HEARTS OF PALM, AND CORN ⟶ ② SIMMER AND SERVE

BEEF STROGANOFF

This classic Russian dish with a rich creamy sauce is a quick alternative to a stew. It works particularly well with pasta, but you could pair it with rice or mashed potatoes instead.

SERVES 4 • READY IN 20 mins

INGREDIENTS

- 4 tbsp olive oil
- 14oz (400g) steak, such as sirloin, very thinly sliced
- 1 onion, finely chopped
- 5½oz (150g) button mushrooms, sliced
- 1 tbsp butter
- 2 tbsp all-purpose flour
- 1¼ cups beef stock
- 4 heaping tbsp crème fraîche or sour cream
- 1 heaping tsp paprika
- salt and freshly ground black pepper
- ½ tbsp lemon juice
- 1 tbsp chopped dill (optional)
- buttered tagliatelle, to serve

1 SEAR THE STEAK AND SET ASIDE

Heat 2 tbsp of the oil in a large, deep-sided frying pan. Sear the steak in batches over high heat, cooking until it just colors. Set aside.

2 COOK THE ONION AND MUSHROOMS

Heat the remaining 2 tbsp of oil in the pan and cook the onion and mushrooms over medium heat for 5 minutes until the mushrooms are golden brown, making sure not to burn the onions.

3 ADD THE STOCK AND THICKEN THE SAUCE

Add the butter and sprinkle with the flour, stirring it in. Gradually stir in the stock and cook for a few minutes until the sauce thickens. Stir in the crème fraîche and paprika and season to taste.

4 RETURN THE BEEF AND SERVE

Return the beef and heat it through. Add the lemon with the dill (if using). Serve over buttered tagliatelle.

PLAN OF ACTION!
1 SEAR STEAK → 2 COOK ONION AND MUSHROOMS → 3 ADD STOCK AND THICKEN SAUCE → 4 RETURN BEEF AND SERVE

MARGHERITA IN MINUTES

This homemade margherita can be ready in less time than it takes for takeout to arrive, and will taste much better! Add extra toppings if you'd like.

MAKES 4 • **READY IN** 20 mins, plus rising (optional)

- 3 cups all-purpose or bread flour, plus extra for dusting
- ¼oz (7g) packet of fast-acting dried yeast
- pinch of salt
- ¼ cup olive oil, plus extra for greasing

FOR THE TOPPING
- 2–3 tbsp tomato paste or sauce
- 5½oz (150g) mozzarella, sliced into thin rounds
- handful of fresh basil leaves, torn

MAKE THE DOUGH

1 SIFT

SIEVE

flour

salt

dried yeast

Sift the flour into a large bowl and add the dried yeast and salt.

2 MIX

warm water

olive oil

Make a well in the mixture.

Slowly add 1½ cups warm water. Mix, adding in the olive oil gradually, until it forms a soft dough.

KNEAD THE DOUGH

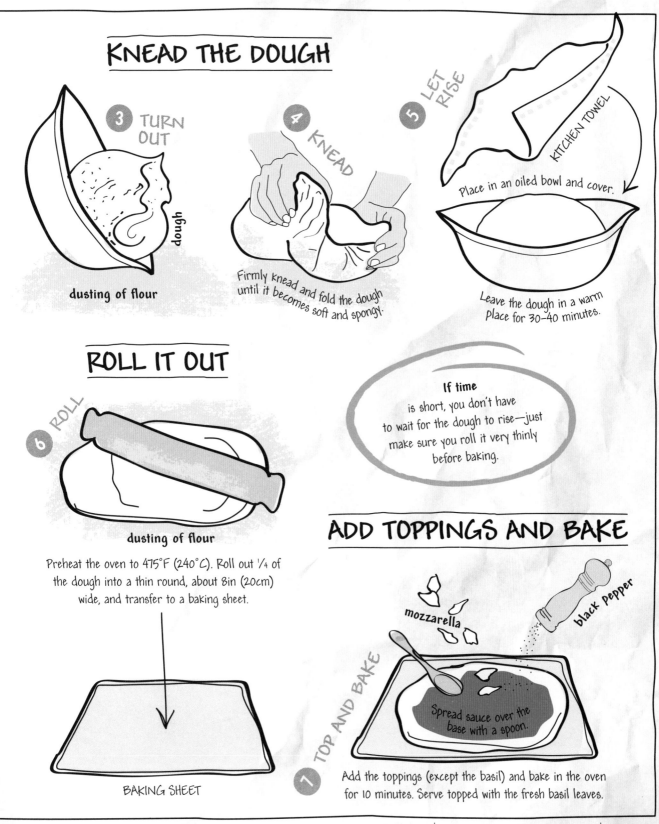

3 TURN OUT

dough

dusting of flour

4 KNEAD

Firmly knead and fold the dough until it becomes soft and spongy.

5 LET RISE

KITCHEN TOWEL

Place in an oiled bowl and cover.

Leave the dough in a warm place for 30–40 minutes.

ROLL IT OUT

6 ROLL

dusting of flour

Preheat the oven to 475°F (240°C). Roll out ¼ of the dough into a thin round, about 8in (20cm) wide, and transfer to a baking sheet.

BAKING SHEET

If time
is short, you don't have to wait for the dough to rise—just make sure you roll it very thinly before baking.

ADD TOPPINGS AND BAKE

mozzarella

black pepper

7 TOP AND BAKE

Spread sauce over the base with a spoon.

Add the toppings (except the basil) and bake in the oven for 10 minutes. Serve topped with the fresh basil leaves.

PIZZA TOPPER

START

1 BASE

TRADITIONAL – see pages 152–3 for the recipe.

FLATBREAD – use a store-bought tortilla, naan, pita, or other flatbread.

2 SAUCE

TOMATO – combine ¼ cup tomato sauce, 1 crushed garlic clove, and 1 tbsp of extra virgin olive oil.

SPICY TOMATO – add 1 tsp dried red pepper flakes to the recipe above.

BBQ SAUCE – see page 68 for the recipe.

BIANCO – melt 2 tbsp butter in a medium pan and stir in 3 tbsp flour. Cook over medium heat, stirring constantly, for 3–4 minutes. Slowly whisk in 1 cup milk. Simmer for 5 minutes, or until thickened, then stir in a large handful of grated Parmesan cheese.

PESTO – see pages 136–7 for recipes.

3 CHEESE

MOZZARELLA – 1 ball or 4½oz (125g) mozzarella pearls, torn.

CHEDDAR – 10oz (300g), grated.

FETA – 7oz (200g), crumbled.

GOAT CHEESE – 7oz (200g), sliced into rounds.

BLUE CHEESE – 5½oz (150g), crumbled.

5 VEGGIES

MARINATED ARTICHOKE HEARTS – 1¾oz (50g), drained.

OLIVES – 1¾oz (50g), sliced.

JALAPEÑO PEPPERS – 1¾oz (50g), sliced.

ROASTED GARLIC – 5 cloves.

CARAMELIZED ONIONS – 7oz (200g).

RED ONION or **SHALLOTS** – 3½oz (100g), thinly sliced.

MUSHROOMS – 3½oz (100g), sliced.

BELL PEPPERS or **ROASTED BELL PEPPERS** – 3½oz (100g), thinly sliced.

EGGPLANT – 2½oz (75g), sliced and broiled.

ZUCCHINI – 3½oz (100g), finely sliced.

ASPARAGUS – 2½oz (75g), shaved into fine slices using a vegetable peeler.

CORN – ½ small can, drained.

AND/OR

4 FRUIT

CHERRY TOMATOES – 3½oz (100g), halved.

SUN-DRIED TOMATOES – 1¾oz (50g), chopped or quartered.

APPLES or **PEARS** – 5½oz (150g), thinly sliced.

PEACHES – 3½oz (100g), sliced.

FRESH FIGS – 7oz (200g), sliced.

PINEAPPLE CHUNKS – 3½oz (100g).

GRAPES – 3½oz (100g), halved.

Once you've mastered the margherita (see pp152–3), it's time to put your speedy pizza skills to the test with our pizza topper flowchart! Simply follow the steps below to mix and match your favorite ingredients. Try not to overload your pizza with toppings, though, as the crust will take longer to cook through.

AND/OR

❻ PROTEIN

PEPPERONI – 7oz (200g).
PROSCIUTTO – 5½oz (150g).
HAM – 5½oz (150g).
ITALIAN SAUSAGE – 9oz (250g).
CHORIZO – 5½oz (150g).
PANCETTA – 3½oz (100g).
CHICKEN BREAST – 5½oz (150g), broiled and shredded.
SHRIMP – 7oz (200g).
TUNA – ½ can, flaked.
ANCHOVIES – 6–8, drained.
EGGS – 4, cracked on top 6–8 minutes before the end of cooking.
WALNUTS – 1 handful, crushed.
PINE NUTS – 1 handful.

❼ SEASONINGS

DRIED HERBS, such as oregano, basil, rosemary, or thyme – 2 tbsp, sprinkled over.
GARLIC POWDER – 1 tsp, sprinkled over.
PAPRIKA – 1 tsp, sprinkled over.
SMOKED PAPRIKA – ½ tsp, sprinkled over.
RED PEPPER FLAKES – ½ tsp, sprinkled over.
BLACK PEPPER – freshly ground.

❽ OILS

OLIVE OIL, MELTED BUTTER, or **MELTED COCONUT OIL** – 1 tbsp brushed onto the crust and drizzled over the pizza before baking.
TRUFFLE OIL, CHILE OIL, or **GARLIC OIL** – 1 tsp drizzled over the baked pizza before serving.

DIPS AND SAUCES

SOUR CREAM • GARLIC MAYO • SMOKY AÏOLI • BLUE CHEESE SAUCE • BALSAMIC GLAZE • TAPENADE • SWEET CHILI SAUCE
(See also pages 166–7 and 200–1.)

FINISH

❾ GARNISHES

PARMESAN – 1¾oz (50g), grated or shaved over the baked pizza before serving.
FRESH BASIL – 1 handful, torn.
RICOTTA CHEESE – 3½oz (100g), spooned over.
AVOCADO – 1, sliced.

INGREDIENTS

1 tsp smoked paprika

1 tsp cayenne pepper

1 tsp garlic powder

½ tsp dried thyme

1 tsp light
brown sugar

½ tsp salt

4 skinless salmon fillets,
approx. 5½oz (150g) each

2 tbsp olive oil

PLAN OF ACTION!

1 GRIND SPICES → **2** PREPARE SALMON → **3** BROIL SALMON

CAJUN-SPICED SALMON

This simple, Louisiana-inspired rub instantly livens up any fish, and it's particularly good with salmon. You can serve the salmon with a thinly-sliced onion, avocado, and cherry tomato salad for a light, flavorful dinner.

SERVES 4 • READY IN 15 mins

- -

1 GRIND THE SPICES

Combine the spices, thyme, sugar, and salt in a mortar and pestle or a spice grinder. Grind to a fine powder.

2 PREPARE THE SALMON

Rub the mixture over both sides of the fish, cover with plastic wrap, and let rest in the fridge while you prepare the broiler.

3 BROIL THE SALMON

Preheat the broiler to its highest setting and line a grill pan with foil. Brush the fish with a little oil on both sides, being careful not to dislodge the spice rub, and broil for 3–4 minutes on each side, depending on thickness.

TIP – The salmon can be marinated in the rub and frozen, uncooked. Defrost thoroughly before cooking from the start of step 3. You can also double the quantity of spice rub and seal the remainder in an airtight container for future use.

This spice rub is great for seasoning chicken, potato, or sweet potato wedges as well as fish.

THE PERFECT STEAK

Good-quality steak needs very little embellishment. Simply pan-frying it in butter with a little salt and pepper will give you perfect results in an instant.

SERVES 2 • **READY IN** 6–14 mins, plus resting

- 1–2 tbsp butter, softened
- 2 x 1½in (3cm) thick beef sirloin or rib-eye steaks
- salt and freshly ground black pepper

> **For rare,** cook for 6–8 minutes in total.
> **For medium,** cook for 10–12 minutes in total.
> **For well done,** cook for 12–14 minutes in total.
> (The thickness of the steak will affect the cooking time.)

COOK THE STEAK

1 ADD

HEAVY-BOTTOMED FRYING PAN

TONGS

butter

steak

Heat the butter over high heat until it simmers, then add the steak.

2 SEAR

SLOTTED SPATULA

Press down on the steak with a slotted spatula, reduce the heat slightly, and sear for 1–2 minutes.

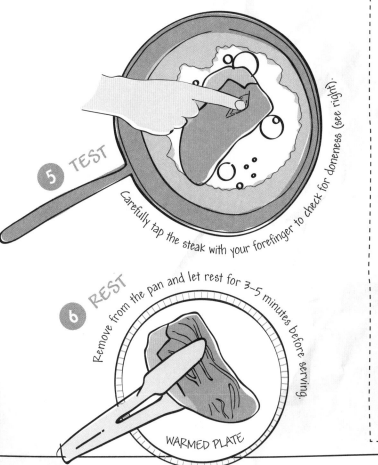

3 CHECK

Lift the steak to check if the underside is well browned.

4 TURN

salt

pepper

Turn the steak and brown the other side. Season the browned side with salt and pepper. Continue to cook the steak, turning every 1–2 minutes, until cooked to your liking.

TEST AND REST

5 TEST

Carefully tap the steak with your forefinger to check for doneness (see right).

6 REST

Remove from the pan and let rest for 3–5 minutes before serving.

WARMED PLATE

TESTING FOR DONENESS

1. Rare Hold your hand with the fingers extended gently forward. Prod the muscle between thumb and forefinger. This is how a rare steak should feel.

2. Medium Stretch out your fingers as far as they will go. Now prod between thumb and forefinger. This is how a medium steak should feel.

3. Well-done Clench your fist tightly and prod between thumb and forefinger. The muscle feels much firmer; this is how well-done meat should feel.

INGREDIENTS

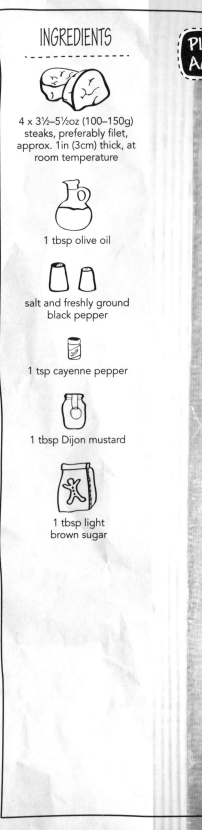

4 x 3½–5½oz (100–150g) steaks, preferably filet, approx. 1in (3cm) thick, at room temperature

1 tbsp olive oil

salt and freshly ground black pepper

1 tsp cayenne pepper

1 tbsp Dijon mustard

1 tbsp light brown sugar

PLAN OF ACTION!

1. **COOK STEAKS** → 2. **ADD GLAZE** → 3. **FINISH UNDER BROILER**

STEAK GLAZED WITH MUSTARD AND BROWN SUGAR

A simple, piquant steak dish makes for a super-quick weeknight meal. Why not throw together a tomato salad while the steaks are cooking? If you've got a little more time, you can bake some sweet potato fries to serve on the side.

SERVES 4 • READY IN 15 mins

1 SEASON AND COOK THE STEAKS

Rub the steaks with the oil and season well with salt, pepper, and cayenne pepper. Cook or grill over high heat until cooked to your liking. For rare, allow 2–3 minutes each side; for medium, 3–4 minutes each side; and for well done, 4–5 minutes each side. Let the meat rest for about 5 minutes, loosely covered with foil to keep warm.

2 ADD THE GLAZE

Meanwhile, preheat the broiler to its highest setting. Brush each steak on 1 side with a thin layer of mustard, then sprinkle with an even layer of the sugar.

3 FINISH UNDER THE BROILER

Broil the steaks for a minute or two only, until the sugar has melted and caramelized over the top. You don't want to cook them any further, just enough to create a lovely glazed effect.

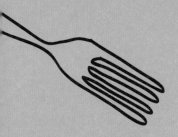

FOOD FOR FRIENDS
WITHOUT THE FUSS

CITRUS-MARINATED OLIVES

Serve these zesty olives alongside dips and flatbreads for your guests to dig in. Make this a few days in advance to allow the flavors of the olives, fruits, spices, and herbs to mingle and infuse.

SERVES 6–8 • **READY IN** 12 mins, plus marinating

INGREDIENTS

- 1 tsp fennel seeds
- ½ tsp cumin seeds
- 9oz (250g) pitted black or green olives, or a mix of both
- grated zest of ½ orange
- grated zest of ½ lemon
- 2 garlic cloves, finely chopped
- 2 tsp red pepper flakes, crushed
- 1 tsp dried oregano
- 1 tbsp lemon juice
- 1 tbsp red wine vinegar
- 2 tbsp olive oil
- 1 tbsp finely chopped flat-leaf parsley

1 TOAST THE SEEDS
Toast the fennel and cumin seeds in a dry pan over low heat for 2 minutes, until aromatic.

2 MARINATE THE OLIVES
Combine the olives, toasted seeds, citrus zests, garlic, red pepper flakes, oregano, lemon juice, vinegar, and oil and toss to coat the olives well. Place in an airtight container. Let marinate at room temperature for at least 8 hours.

3 SHAKE AND GARNISH
Shake the container occasionally to coat the ingredients while marinating. Stir in the parsley up to 3 hours before serving, and serve at room temperature.

TIP – Warming the olives will intensify the flavors of this dish. If you have time, gently heat them in a frying pan for about 5 minutes, until warmed through, and serve warm.

PLAN OF ACTION! 1 TOAST SEEDS → 2 MARINATE OLIVES → 3 SHAKE AND GARNISH

FIG AND GOAT CHEESE TOASTS

These toasts combine the freshness of figs with creamy soft goat cheese and aromatic honey. A great combo for the perfect summer mezze dish.

SERVES 6 • **READY IN** 20 mins

INGREDIENTS

- 1 baguette
- 8 ripe figs
- 9oz (250g) fresh goat cheese
- 6–8 tbsp rosemary or lavender honey

1 TOAST THE BAGUETTE

Preheat the broiler. Half the baguette lengthwise and slice each half into smaller pieces. Arrange them in one layer on a baking sheet and lightly toast them on both sides under the broiler.

2 TOP WITH FIGS AND CHEESE

Slice the figs lengthwise. Arrange on top of the toasted baguette slices. Spoon over the goat cheese, pressing it down a little.

3 BROIL THE TOASTS

Place under the broiler for 3–4 minutes until bubbling and a little golden.

4 DRIZZLE AND SERVE

Drizzle with the honey and serve immediately.

As an alternative to rosemary or lavender honey, use plain honey and sprinkle the toasts with your herb of choice.

PLAN OF ACTION!

1 TOAST BAGUETTE → **2 TOP WITH FIGS AND CHEESE** → **3 BROIL TOASTS** → **4 DRIZZLE AND SERVE**

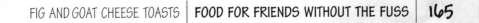

DIPS ON THE DOUBLE

Cilantro jalapeño hummus

Blend 1 can of **navy beans** with 1 tbsp **tahini**, 1 **jalapeño** (seeded), **onion**, **cilantro**, **olive oil**, **lime juice**, **garlic**, and **red pepper flakes**.

You can substitute **black-eyed peas** for the black beans in this dip.

Black bean dip

Blend 1 can of **black beans** (drained) with **red onion**, **lime juice**, **olive oil**, **garlic**, **hot smoked paprika**, and **cilantro**.

Sun-dried tomato dip

Purée 1 jar of **sun-dried tomatoes** (including the oil) with **onion**, **garlic**, **olive oil**, **balsamic vinegar**, **basil**, and **dried oregano**.

Sweet potato hummus

Purée 1 cooked **sweet potato** with ½ can of **chickpeas**, 1 tbsp **tahini**, **red onion**, **garlic**, **olive oil**, and **salt**.

Dips are great for when you've got friends over. The quantities here serve 4 as an appetizer, so adjust as needed. Allow ½–1 onion and 1–2 garlic cloves (crushed) per dip, and season to taste. Use a food processor to purée the dips on page 166 into a paste; the recipes on this page can be chopped or mashed by hand with a knife or fork.

Spinach artichoke dip

Use a Knife to finely chop the olives, anchovies, and capers before adding the wet ingredients, or **use a food processor** to purée this dip into a paste.

Tapenade

Mix a couple of handfuls of fresh **spinach** (wilted and drained) with a jar of **artichokes** (drained), 4oz (115g) each of **cream cheese** and **sour cream**, grated **Parmesan**, **red pepper flakes**, **salt**, and **garlic powder**.

Purée 1 jar of pitted **black olives** (drained) and a few **anchovies** with **garlic**, **capers**, **basil**, **olive oil**, and **lemon juice**.

Traditional guacamole

To serve, drizzle with **chili sauce**.

Smoked fish dip

Mash together 3 **avocados** with **lime juice**, **salt**, **cayenne pepper**, and **red pepper flakes**. Fold in **garlic**, chopped **cherry tomatoes**, and **cilantro**.

Mix 2 fillets of flaked **smoked fish** with 4oz (115g) **cream cheese**, 1 tbsp **mayo**, and **lemon juice**. Fold in chopped **celery**, **jalapeño**, **gherkin**, **onion**, and **parsley**.

DIPPERS AND SNACK HACKS

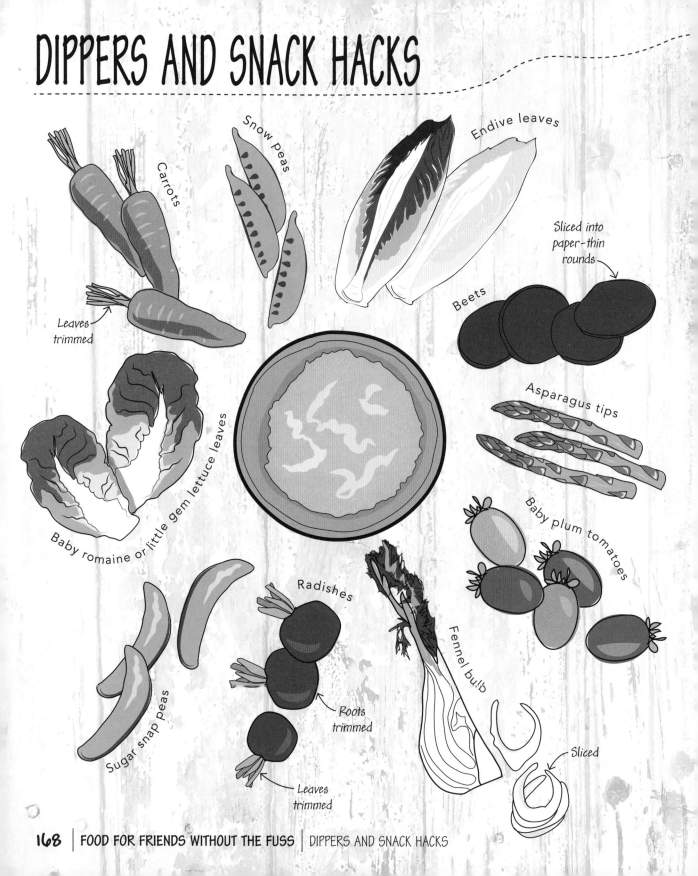

Snow peas

Endive leaves

Carrots

Leaves trimmed

Sliced into paper-thin rounds

Beets

Asparagus tips

Baby romaine or little gem lettuce leaves

Baby plum tomatoes

Radishes

Roots trimmed

Fennel bulb

Sliced

Sugar snap peas

Leaves trimmed

Now that you've made your delicious dips (see pp166–7), what will you serve them with? The no-cook crudités on page 168 make for an impressive platter, while the snack hacks below are the perfect homemade alternative to store-bought bites. They're sure to keep your guests happy!

Crostini

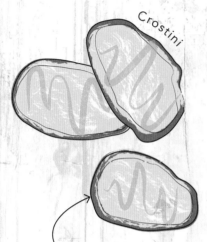

Preheat the oven to 350°F (180°C). Cut a baguette into slices, brush them with olive oil, then season with salt and pepper. Bake for 10–15 minutes, or until golden.

Herbed flatbread crisps

Preheat the oven to 400°F (200°C). Make a dough (see pp152–3, steps 1–4) and roll it out very thinly on a clean, flour-dusted surface. Brush with olive oil, scatter with dried herbs, and cut into segments. Transfer to a baking sheet, then bake for about 10 minutes, or until lightly browned.

Mixed root tempura also make great dippers! See pp178–9.

Preheat the oven to 350°F (180°C). Spoon heaping tablespoons of grated Parmesan cheese into mounds on a baking sheet lined with parchment paper. Bake for 8–10 minutes, or until golden brown and slightly toasted. Transfer to a wire rack to cool.

Parmesan thins

Why not try serving breadsticks wrapped in Prosciutto alongside your homemade dippers? See pp188–9.

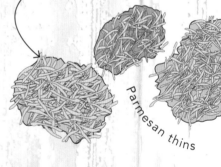

Preheat the oven to 375°F (190°C). Slice your choice of sweet potatoes, parsnips, beets, or potatoes as thinly as possible (use a mandolin slicer, if you have one). Toss the vegetables with olive oil and bake for 15–20 minutes, or until crisp. Serve sprinkled with salt.

Tortilla chips

Preheat the oven to 400°F (200°C). Brush both sides of some corn tortillas with vegetable oil, then cut into triangles. Arrange in a single layer on a baking sheet, and bake for 7–8 minutes, or until golden and crispy. Serve sprinkled with salt.

Vegetable chips

FRIED HALLOUMI

Halloumi is a firm, slightly springy white cheese traditionally made from sheep and goat's milk. It's salty-savory flavor pairs well as a mezze with harissa paste, hummus, or a green salad with red onion.

SERVES 4-6 • **READY IN 8-10 mins**

INGREDIENTS

- 2 x 9oz (250g) packages halloumi cheese
- flour, for dusting
- ½ cup olive oil, plus extra for drizzling
- 2 handfuls of thyme or oregano leaves
- juice of 2 lemons
- 1 lemon, cut into wedges, to serve

❶ PREPARE THE HALLOUMI

Rinse the halloumi cheese before using to rid it of excess salt; dry well on paper towels. Cut the halloumi into ½in (1cm) thick slices and dust lightly with flour.

❷ FRY THE HALLOUMI

Heat the oil in a non-stick frying pan over high heat and fry the cheese for 2–3 minutes on each side, or until golden brown.

❸ SEASON, GARNISH, AND SERVE

Remove from the pan and sprinkle with the thyme and lemon juice. Serve immediately with a little oil drizzled over and lemon wedges on the side.

Halloumi goes well with many dishes. You could try it with salsa criolla (see p146), inside a bun with a bean burger (see p100), or in place of goat cheese in a bulgur wheat and pepper salad (see p98).

PLAN OF ACTION! ❶ PREPARE HALLOUMI → ❷ FRY HALLOUMI → ❸ SEASON, GARNISH, AND SERVE

MOROCCAN-STYLE SHRIMP

Originally from Morocco, this easy dish tastes as good as it smells. Serve tapas-style with toothpicks or forks, perhaps with some crème fraîche for dipping.

SERVES 4-6 • **READY IN** 10 mins

INGREDIENTS

- 1lb 2oz (500g) uncooked peeled large shrimp (defrosted if frozen)
- ¼ cup olive oil
- ½ tsp harissa paste or hot paprika
- 1 tsp ground ginger
- 1 tsp ground cumin
- ½ tsp ground coriander
- 3 garlic cloves, crushed
- 1 tbsp snipped flat-leaf parsley
- 1 tbsp snipped cilantro

1 PREPARE THE SHRIMP

Drain the shrimp on a double layer of paper towels.

2 COOK THE GARLIC AND SPICES

Heat the oil in a large frying pan, pour in the spices and garlic, and stir for a minute to release the flavors.

3 COOK THE SHRIMP

Add the shrimp and cook for 1–2 minutes over medium-high heat until they turn a little pink, then turn over. Cook until the shrimp are pink all over, stirring frequently.

4 GARNISH AND SERVE

Stir in the fresh parsley and cilantro and serve hot.

TIP – To prepare an unpeeled, uncooked shrimp, pull off the head, then carefully peel away the shell, starting from the underside. Discard both, or use for stock. Next, remove the dark vein. Lay the shrimp flat and, using a small, sharp knife, make an incision down the back of the shrimp and pull out the vein. Repeat for the remaining shrimp and follow the method from step 1. Always wash your hands before and after preparing shrimp, and thoroughly clean any kitchen equipment used.

PLAN OF ACTION!

1 PREPARE SHRIMP → 2 COOK GARLIC AND SPICES → 3 COOK SHRIMP → 4 GARNISH AND SERVE

QUICK PICKLES

These are the homemade equivalent of gherkins, with a crunchier texture and punchier taste. They're delicious served as a side, or with charcuterie or cheese.

MAKES 2 jars • **READY IN** 10 mins, plus sterilizing and chilling

SPECIAL EQUIPMENT 2 x 7fl oz (200ml) jars

- ¼ cup granulated sugar
- 2 tsp salt
- ¾ cup white wine vinegar or rice wine vinegar
- freshly ground black pepper

- 4–5 small cucumbers or 1 large cucumber, thinly sliced
- 1 tbsp finely chopped dill fronds
- ½ tsp dill seeds, lightly crushed

STERILIZE THE JARS

It's important to sterilize the jars so that your pickles don't become contaminated and turn moldy. Allow the jars to cool before you fill them.

1 HEAT JARS

BAKING SHEET

GLASS JARS

Wash the jars, place them upside-down on a baking sheet, and put in an oven, preheated to 275°F (140°C), for at least 15 minutes.

boiling water

METAL BOWL

2 BOIL LIDS

Pour boiling water over the lids and leave for 5 minutes. Remove and drain.

MAKE THE VINEGAR MIX

salt

sugar

black pepper

WHISK

vinegar

3 COMBINE

Whisk the sugar and salt with a little vinegar until dissolved. Add the remaining vinegar and a good grinding of black pepper.

PACK INTO JARS

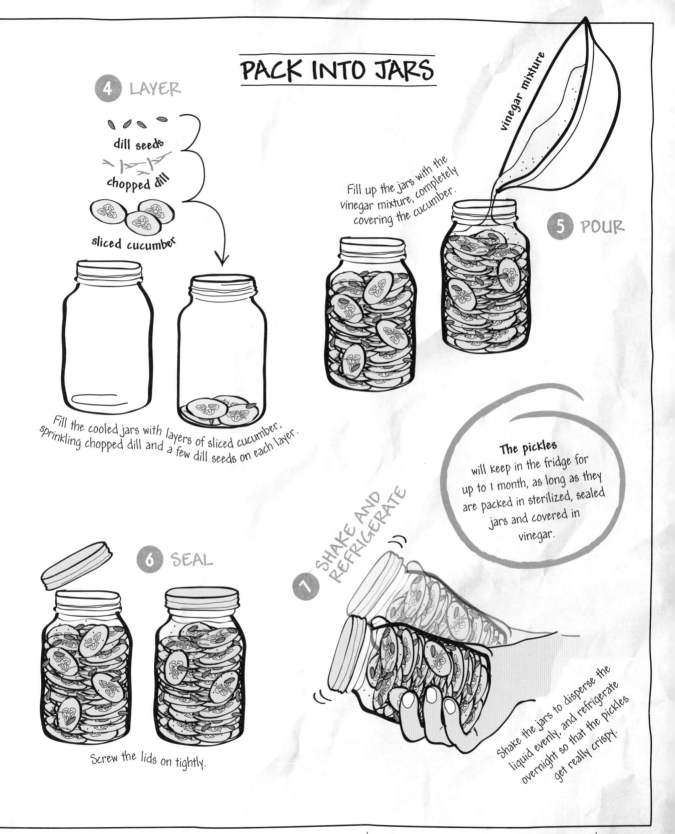

④ LAYER

dill seeds

chopped dill

sliced cucumber

Fill the cooled jars with layers of sliced cucumber, sprinkling chopped dill and a few dill seeds on each layer.

vinegar mixture

Fill up the jars with the vinegar mixture, completely covering the cucumber.

⑤ POUR

The pickles
will keep in the fridge for up to 1 month, as long as they are packed in sterilized, sealed jars and covered in vinegar.

⑥ SEAL

Screw the lids on tightly.

⑦ SHAKE AND REFRIGERATE

Shake the jars to disperse the liquid evenly, and refrigerate overnight so that the pickles get really crispy.

THE PERFECT CHEESEBOARD

THE CHEESES

It's important to provide a range of flavors and textures to tickle the tastebuds and keep everyone happy—try some out first to find your favorites! Allow around 2oz (55g) of each cheese per person, and serve at room temperature.

1 MILD-TASTING
Edam is a semi-soft cheese with a sweet, buttery flavor.
Try also: Gouda, taleggio, Jarlsberg, or Wensleydale.

2 STRONG-TASTING
Stilton is a smooth-textured, sharp-tasting blue cheese.
Try also: Roquefort, Gorgonzola, or Bleu d'Auvergne.

3 SOFT
Camembert is a soft white cheese with a creamy texture.
Try also: Brie, Brillat-Savarin, chèvre, or Stinking Bishop.

4 HARD
Manchego has the nutty taste of aromatic sheep's milk.
Try also: Cheddar, Emmental, Caerphilly, or pecorino.

THE ACCOMPANIMENTS

The right accompaniments will bring out the flavors of your cheeses, as well as cleansing the palate between mouthfuls.

5 CHUTNEY/JAM/PRESERVES
Try: **fig jam**, **honey**, red onion chutney, or plum chutney.

6 NUTS
Try: **smoked almonds**, cashews, or pickled walnuts.

7 FRESH FRUIT
Try: **apples**, pears, grapes, figs, or blackberries.

8 PICKLES
Try: **cornichons**, gherkins, pickled onions, or piccalilli.

9 SPREAD/RELISH
Try: **olive tapenade** (see p167), or plum or quince paste.

10 BREADS
Try: **sourdough bread**, crackers, or ciabatta.

When assembling your cheeseboard, aim for a carefully balanced selection of cheeses and accompaniments. This will give your guests lots of choice and allow them to create their own favorite combinations. If you're including a cheeseboard as part of a full meal, serve it after the main course but before dessert.

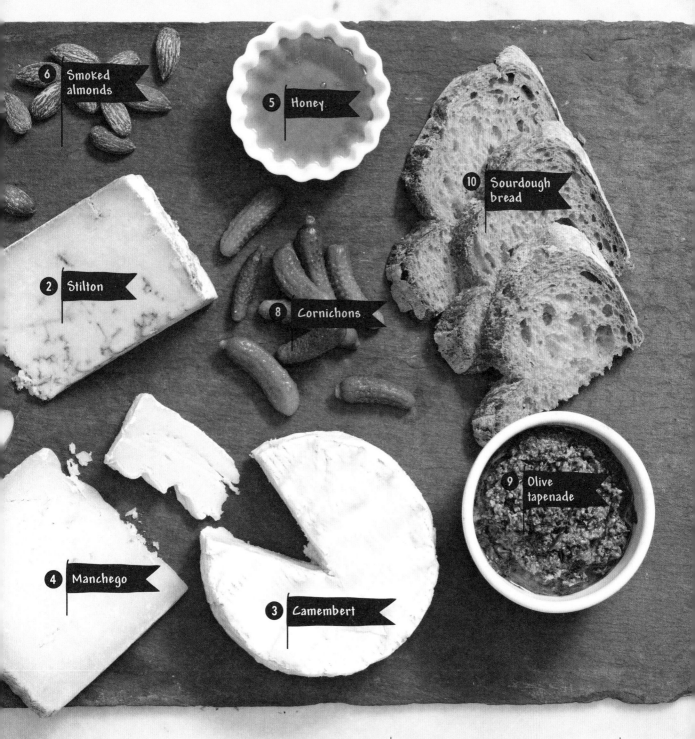

6 Smoked almonds

5 Honey

10 Sourdough bread

2 Stilton

8 Cornichons

9 Olive tapenade

4 Manchego

3 Camembert

SPEEDY SEAFOOD CEVICHE

Ceviche is a sophisticated-looking dish to serve to your guests as an appetizer or light snack. The brief, light pickling of raw fish brings out its natural flavors by "cooking" it with lemon juice—make sure you use only the freshest fish!

SERVES 4 • **READY IN** 20 mins, plus chilling

1 SLICE THE FISH
With a sharp knife, cut the fish into small, evenly sized cubes.

2 PREPARE THE MARINADE
Spread the onion evenly in the bottom of a shallow, non-metallic dish. Pour in the lemon juice and olive oil, then sprinkle with the paprika and chile.

3 ADD THE FISH
Place the fish on the onion, gently turning to coat with the marinade. Cover and marinate in the refrigerator for 15–20 minutes. Season with salt and pepper, sprinkle with parsley, and serve with crusty bread.

TIP – The fish will be much easier to slice if you put it in the freezer for a few minutes first. The ceviche can be assembled, covered, and chilled up to 2 hours in advance. Return it to room temperature before serving.

Use extremely fresh semi- or firm-fleshed fish in ceviche. Salmon (shown here), halibut, turbot, monkfish, and sea bass all work well.

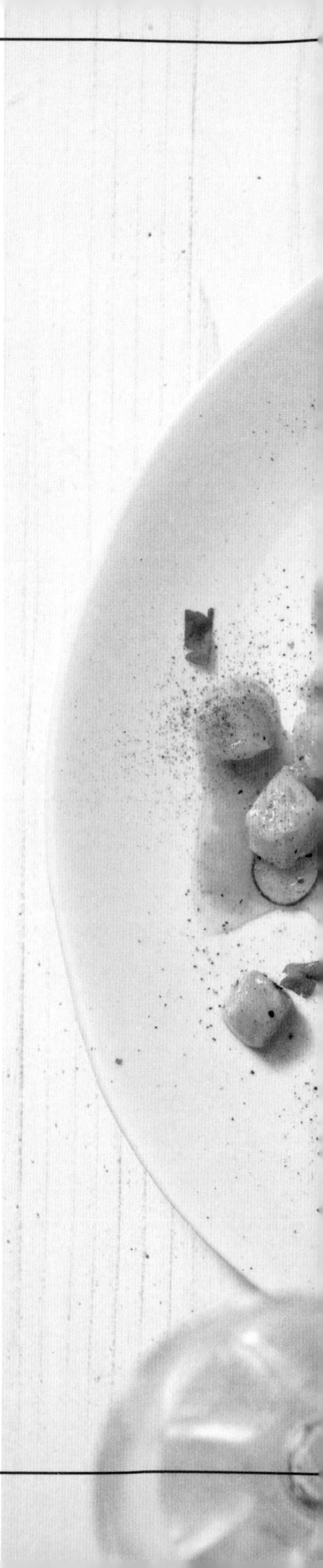

INGREDIENTS

1lb (450g) very fresh, semi- or firm-fleshed fish fillets, pinboned, skinned, and chilled

1 red onion, diced

juice of 2–3 lemons or limes

1 tbsp olive oil

½ tsp hot smoked paprika (pimentón picante)

1 chile, finely chopped

salt and freshly ground black pepper

2 tbsp finely chopped flat-leaf parsley

MIXED ROOT TEMPURA

Root vegetables and leeks are given a Japanese treatment in this quick tempura recipe. Serve to your guests with sweet chili sauce for dipping.

SERVES 4–6 • **READY IN** 20–25 mins

- 1 parsnip, cut into short fingers
- 1 large carrot, cut into short fingers
- ½ small celeriac, cut into small chunks
- ½ small rutabaga
- 1 leek, cut into thick slices
- 2 tbsp cornstarch
- sunflower oil, for deep-frying

FOR THE BATTER
- ½ cup self-rising flour
- ½ cup cornstarch
- ¾ cup sparkling mineral water
- 2 tsp sunflower oil
- ½ tsp salt
- ¾ tsp cumin seeds

PREPARE THE VEGETABLES

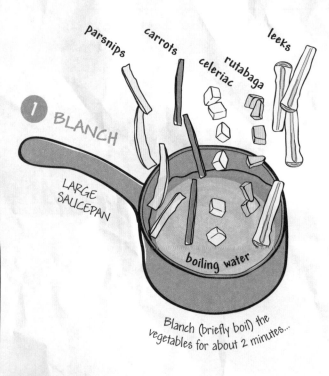

parsnips   carrots   celeriac   rutabaga   leeks

1 BLANCH

LARGE SAUCEPAN

boiling water

Blanch (briefly boil) the vegetables for about 2 minutes...

2 DRAIN

COLANDER

...then drain.

4 COAT — cornstarch

3 DRY

PAPER TOWELS

Sprinkle in the cornstarch and toss to coat.

WHILE YOU FINISH PREPARING THE VEGGIES, HEAT THE OIL IN A LARGE WOK OVER HIGH HEAT.

DEEP FRY IN BATCHES

MAKE THE BATTER

5 WHISK

cornstarch

cumin seeds

vegetable oil

sparkling water

salt

self-rising flour

Whisk the batter ingredients until well combined.

6 DIP

Dip the veggies in the batter, a few at a time, to coat lightly. Shake off any excess.

7 FRY

LARGE WOK

sizzling hot oil

Deep-fry the veg for 2–3 minutes, turning occasionally, until golden.

SLOTTED SPOON

8 DRAIN AND SERVE

PAPER TOWELS

Remove the tempura and drain. Serve hot with dipping sauce.

THE BRUSCHETTA BAR

Sauté the **mushrooms** with a little **butter** and **balsamic vinegar** over high heat for 2 minutes, or until browned.

Balsamic mushrooms with cream cheese

Cream cheese, cucumber, and cherry tomato with snipped chives

For lots of **pesto recipe** ideas, see p136.

Pesto with shavings of Parmesan cheese

Ricotta cheese, raspberries, and honey with fresh mint

Why not wow your guests with a sumptuous selection of bruschetta toppings? Serve the classic Italian appetizers buffet-style, letting your guests help themselves. For the bases, drizzle thin slices of baguette with olive oil and broil until crisp on both sides.

Freshly ground **black pepper**

Tomato, mozzarella, and fresh basil

Chopped pitted olives and preserved red peppers with creamy goat cheese

Toss the halved **strawberries** in **balsamic vinegar.**

Diced mango and avocado with fresh cilantro

Strawberries and balsamic vinegar with burrata cheese

INGREDIENTS

14oz (400g) store-bought
puff pastry

2 tbsp red pesto

3 medium tomatoes,
sliced

2–3 tbsp harissa paste
(optional)

1 tbsp olive oil

3½oz (100g) feta cheese

few sprigs of fresh thyme,
leaves picked

FETA, TOMATO, AND RED PESTO TART

This is a stylish-looking meal that's easy to whip up while your guests are chatting over drinks and appetizers, and it's suitable for vegetarians, too! For a finishing touch, try serving it with arugula on top or a green salad on the side.

SERVES 6 • **READY IN** 20 mins

1 PREPARE THE PASTRY

Preheat the oven to 400°F (200°C). Roll out the pastry on a floured work surface, into a large rectangle or square. Lay a baking sheet on top, then use a sharp knife to score a border about 2in (5cm) in from the edges all the way around, being careful not to cut all the way through the pastry. Next, using the back of the knife, score the pastry around the outer edges—this will help it to puff up.

2 ASSEMBLE THE TART

Working inside the border, smother the pastry with the pesto. Arrange the tomatoes on top, cut-side up. Mix the harissa, if using, with the olive oil, and drizzle over the tomatoes. Crumble over the feta cheese and scatter with the thyme leaves.

3 BAKE TO PERFECTION

Bake the tart in the oven for about 15 minutes or until the pastry is cooked and golden. Serve hot.

You can have fun mixing and matching lots of different toppings for this tart. Why not try adding anchovies, olives, or marinated artichokes? Basil works well instead of thyme, and chile or garlic oil can be used in place of harissa. Also, if you've made your own pesto (see pp136–37), this tart is ideal for showing it off!

POTSTICKER DUMPLINGS

These Chinese-style dumplings are pan-fried for a browned, crunchy exterior and then steamed to cook the filling. Serve with soy sauce or sweet chili sauce.

MAKES 36 • **READY IN 20–30 mins**

FOR THE FILLING
- 1lb (450g) ground pork
- 3½oz (100g) cabbage, shredded
- 3½oz (100g) onion, finely chopped
- 1¾oz (50g) fresh ginger, finely chopped
- 3½oz (100g) scallions, chopped
- 3 garlic cloves, crushed
- 2 tsp sesame oil
- 1 tbsp hoisin sauce
- 2 tbsp rice wine

FOR THE WRAPPERS
- 36 wonton wrappers
- 1 tsp sesame oil
- all-purpose flour, for dusting

> **For a veggie filling**, use 14oz (400g) finely chopped shiitake mushrooms instead of the pork, omit the onion and ginger, halve the amount of scallions and sesame oil, and add a tsp of salt and 1¾oz (50g) finely chopped cilantro.

MAKE THE FILLING

1 COMBINE

cabbage, onion, ginger, scallions, crushed garlic, sesame oil, hoisin sauce, rice wine

ground pork

Place all the ingredients for the filling in a large bowl and mix well to combine.

FORM THE DUMPLINGS

dusting of flour

2 FILL

Fill with mixture

wonton wrappers

Lay the wonton wrappers on a lightly floured surface. Place 1 tablespoon of the filling in the center of each wrapper.

3 FOLD AND SEAL

water

Use your finger to dampen the edges of the wrappers with water.

Fold the wrappers in half, over the filling, to form a triangle.

Use your fingers to press and seal the edges together.

COOK, STEAM, AND SERVE

4 COOK

Heat the oil over medium heat.

LARGE NONSTICK FRYING PAN

Add the dumplings, in batches, and cook for 1–2 minutes on each side, until browned.

5 STEAM

water

FRYING PAN LID

Add ¼ cup of water to the pan, cover, and steam for 3–5 minutes. Remove and serve immediately.

To save time, prepare the dumplings in batches, forming the second batch while the first is cooking, and so on.

DEVILED EGGS

These easy-to-prepare boiled eggs with spiced yolks are great crowd-pleasers. Just serve them at your next party or take them on a picnic, and watch them disappear!

SERVES 4 • **READY IN** 18 mins

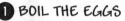

INGREDIENTS

- 6 eggs
- 1 tsp mustard
- 1 tsp hot paprika, plus extra for dusting
- 3 tbsp mayonnaise
- salt and freshly ground black pepper
- 3 cherry tomatoes, cut in quarters
- 1 tbsp chopped chives

❶ BOIL THE EGGS

Place the eggs in a large saucepan and cover with plenty of water. Bring to a boil, then turn down the heat and simmer for about 8 minutes. Carefully remove the eggs and plunge them into cold water, letting them cool. Peel off the shells and cut the eggs in half lengthwise.

❷ MAKE THE YOLK MIXTURE

Remove the yolks and place them in a bowl. Add the mustard, paprika, and mayonnaise, and mash together with a fork until well combined. Season to taste with salt and pepper.

❸ FILL THE EGG WHITES AND SERVE

Divide the yolk mixture between the egg white halves and top each one with a slice of cherry tomato. Sprinkle with the chives, dust with paprika, and serve cold.

Instead of the cherry tomatoes, serve with a range of toppings, such as chopped olives, smoked salmon, bacon bits, or sun-dried tomatoes.

PLAN OF ACTION!
❶ BOIL EGGS → ❷ MAKE YOLK MIXTURE → ❸ FILL EGGS AND SERVE

QUICHE CUPS

These individual quiches are quick and easy to make and are ideal finger food for parties, buffets, and picnics. You'll need a food processor to make short work of the pastry dough and a 12-hole muffin pan to bake the cups in. The quantities given here are for 12 quiche cups.

HOW TO MAKE

- 8 tbsp unsalted butter, chilled and diced, plus extra for greasing
- 1½ cups all-purpose flour
- 1 tsp sugar
- 1 tsp salt
- 6 eggs, beaten
- 1 cup milk

Preheat the oven to 350°F (180°C) and grease the muffin pan.

For the dough, place the butter, flour, sugar, and salt in a food processor and pulse until the mixture resembles bread crumbs. Add ¼ cup of cold water, a little at a time, and bring together to form a dough. Divide the dough and firmly press it into the muffin pan to create a thin crust.

For the filling, place the eggs and milk in a bowl and whisk well to combine. Add the filling (try any of the combinations, right, or experiment with your own) and mix well to combine. Pour the filling into the muffin pan and bake for about 20 minutes, or until the dough is golden and the egg set. Best served hot.

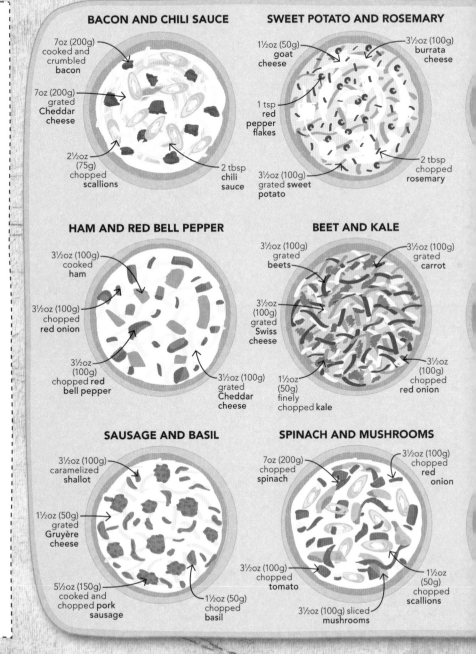

BACON AND CHILI SAUCE

- 7oz (200g) cooked and crumbled bacon
- 7oz (200g) grated Cheddar cheese
- 2½oz (75g) chopped scallions
- 2 tbsp chili sauce

SWEET POTATO AND ROSEMARY

- 1½oz (50g) goat cheese
- 3½oz (100g) burrata cheese
- 1 tsp red pepper flakes
- 3½oz (100g) grated sweet potato
- 2 tbsp chopped rosemary

HAM AND RED BELL PEPPER

- 3½oz (100g) cooked ham
- 3½oz (100g) chopped red onion
- 3½oz (100g) chopped red bell pepper
- 3½oz (100g) grated Cheddar cheese

BEET AND KALE

- 3½oz (100g) grated beets
- 3½oz (100g) grated carrot
- 3½oz (100g) grated Swiss cheese
- 1½oz (50g) finely chopped kale
- 3½oz (100g) chopped red onion

SAUSAGE AND BASIL

- 3½oz (100g) caramelized shallot
- 1½oz (50g) grated Gruyère cheese
- 5½oz (150g) cooked and chopped pork sausage
- 1½oz (50g) chopped basil

SPINACH AND MUSHROOMS

- 7oz (200g) chopped spinach
- 3½oz (100g) chopped red onion
- 3½oz (100g) chopped tomato
- 3½oz (100g) sliced mushrooms
- 1½oz (50g) chopped scallions

THE PERFECT CHARCUTERIE BOARD

A charcuterie board is the ideal pre-dinner fare—great for relaxed, tapas-style snacking alongside drinks. If you include a cheeseboard (see pp174–5), too, you can make the whole meal a sharing experience.

(see pp174–5)

THE MEATS

Pork offers the widest range of cured cuts (although other meats are cured, too). Choose 3 or 4 different meats in total, allowing 3 slices of each meat per person.

1 DRY-CURED MEATS
Aim for a selection of 2–3 dry-cured meats, such as:
Serrano ham – a Spanish "mountain" ham with a sweet taste and chewy texture.
Coppa (or capocollo or capicola) – a well-marbled Italian ham made from pork shoulder or neck.
Prosciutto di parma (or Parma ham) – a famous Italian ham that's sweet, salty, and moist.
Try also: Ibérico ham, bellota, or speck.

2 DRY-CURED SAUSAGES
Include 1–2 dry-cured sausages, such as:
Dry-cured chorizo – a rich Spanish sausage spiced with hot or sweet smoked paprika.
Try also: salchichón, saucisson sec, or salami.

THE ACCOMPANIMENTS

Offer a good selection of accompaniments. Pairing the meats with a range of other tastes and textures will make for interesting flavor combinations.

3 PÂTÉS AND TERRINES
These cooked meats bring a unique texture to the board.
Try either **chicken liver pâté**, pork rillettes, or Brussels pâté.

4 SWEET AND SAVORY SPREADS
Include 1–2 sweet spreads, such as **peach jam** or **honeycomb**, and 1 savory spread, such as **Dijon** or whole-grain mustard.

5 OLIVES AND PICKLES
Pickled vegetables are a must. Include 2–3, such as **green olives**, **pickled onions**, **dill pickles**, or pickled okra.

6 SALAD LEAVES AND HERBS
A simple green salad offers a light and fresh counterpoint to the other strong flavors. Try: **arugula**, mixed baby leaves, or fresh dill.

7 BREADS
Provide an array of breads and crackers, such as **flatbreads**, **breadsticks**, and slices of baguette.

4 Peach jam

3 Chicken liver pâté

4 Dijon mustard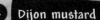

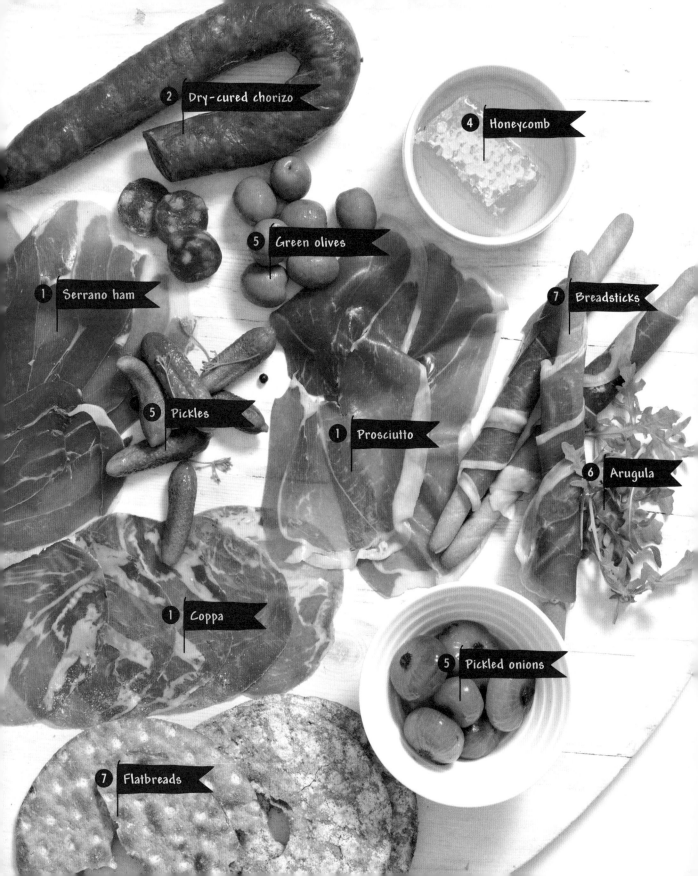

2 Dry-cured chorizo

4 Honeycomb

5 Green olives

1 Serrano ham

7 Breadsticks

5 Pickles

1 Prosciutto

6 Arugula

1 Coppa

5 Pickled onions

7 Flatbreads

SMOKED SALMON AND CRÈME FRAÎCHE SPAGHETTI

A simple yet stylish way to pull together a fabulous dinner with just a few ingredients, this straightforward spaghetti is packed with flavor—dill and salmon are a match made in heaven!

SERVES 4 • **READY IN** 15 mins

INGREDIENTS

- 10oz (300g) dried spaghetti
- salt and freshly ground black pepper
- ¾ cup low-fat crème fraîche
- 4oz (120g) smoked salmon, finely chopped
- 1 tbsp finely chopped capers, rinsed, or more to taste
- finely grated zest of ½ lemon
- 2 tbsp finely chopped dill
- finely grated Parmesan cheese, to serve

1 COOK THE PASTA

Cook the pasta in a large pan of boiling salted water according to the package instructions.

2 MIX THE CRÈME FRAÎCHE AND SALMON

Meanwhile, beat the crème fraîche in a bowl until smooth. Add the smoked salmon, capers, lemon zest, and dill, and season to taste.

3 TOSS, HEAT, AND SERVE

Drain the pasta (reserving a ladleful of the cooking water) and return it to the pan with the reserved water. Toss the sauce through the pasta and return it to the heat, stirring just long enough both for the pasta to soak up some of the sauce and for the sauce to heat through. Loosen the sauce with the reserved cooking water if necessary. Serve with the Parmesan cheese.

PLAN OF ACTION!   1 COOK PASTA → 2 MIX CRÈME FRAÎCHE AND SALMON → 3 TOSS, HEAT, AND SERVE

SAUTÉED SCALLOPS WITH PANCETTA

Treat your friends to a taste of the sea! Scallops are so quick to cook that you've got time to make a rich *jus* (sauce) from pancetta and balsamic vinegar. Serve with pasta or bread for a main meal.

SERVES 4 • **READY IN** 20 mins

INGREDIENTS

- 12 fresh scallops, tough muscle removed (see tip)
- salt and freshly ground black pepper
- 1–2 tbsp olive oil
- 4oz (115g) pancetta, diced
- dash of good-quality thick balsamic vinegar
- 2 handfuls of spinach leaves, stalks removed
- juice of 1 lemon

1 COOK THE SCALLOPS

Pat the scallops dry using paper towels, and season with salt and pepper. Heat the oil in a non-stick frying pan over medium-high heat. When hot, add the scallops, positioning them around the edge of the pan. Sear for 1–2 minutes on one side, then turn them over, starting with the first one you put in the pan. Once you have completed the circle, remove the scallops from the pan (again starting with the first one), and set aside to keep warm.

2 COOK THE PANCETTA AND MAKE THE SAUCE

Cook the pancetta in the same pan and cook for 2–3 minutes or until crispy. Add a generous amount of balsamic vinegar to the pan, increase the heat to high, and let it boil for 2–3 minutes, stirring to deglaze the pan. Then drizzle the sauce over the cooked scallops.

3 WILT THE SPINACH

Still using the same pan, add in the spinach. Cook for 2–3 minutes, moving it around the pan, until it is just wilted. Squeeze over the lemon juice, and serve immediately with the scallops and pancetta sauce.

TIP – Scallops are available pre-prepared at most large supermarkets and fish counters. You may still need to remove the tough muscle attached to the side. Simply peel it off with your fingers before cooking.

PLAN OF ACTION!
1 COOK SCALLOPS → 2 COOK PANCETTA AND MAKE SAUCE → 3 WILT SPINACH

MOULES MARINIÈRES

This classic French dish is a delicious meal to share with friends—you can eat this with your hands, using the empty shells to scoop out the mussel meat.

SERVES 4 • **READY IN** 20 mins

- 8lb (3.6kg) fresh mussels, cleaned
- 4 tbsp butter
- 2 onions, finely chopped
- 2 garlic cloves
- 2 cups dry white wine
- 4 bay leaves
- 2 sprigs of thyme
- salt and freshly ground black pepper
- 2–4 tbsp chopped parsley
- crusty bread, to serve

PREPARE THE MUSSELS

KITCHEN TAP

Scrub the mussels under cold running water using a stiff brush.

1 CLEAN AND SORT

Discard any with broken shells or open ones that don't shut when tapped sharply on the edge of the sink.

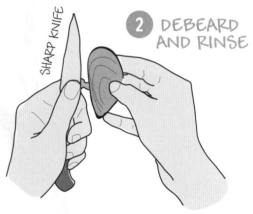

SHARP KNIFE

2 DEBEARD AND RINSE

Pull off the "beards" by tugging each beard sharply away from the shell. Then rinse again.

Mussel "beards" are fibrous threads that mussels use for gripping onto surfaces. They are inedible, so it's important to remove them.

COOK THE DISH

3 SOFTEN

butter and onions

LARGE SAUCEPAN

Heat the butter over medium heat.
Gently cook the onion until softened.

4 COMBINE

salt

bay leaves

mussels

pepper

thyme

wine

garlic

Add the mussels, garlic, wine,
bay leaves, thyme, salt, and pepper.
Increase the heat and bring to a boil.

5 COVER AND COOK

Shake the pan occasionally.

Cover and cook for 5 minutes.

6 GARNISH AND SERVE

parsley

Discard any closed mussels and stir
in the chopped parsley. Serve at once
with chunks of crusty bread.

THAI FISHCAKES

You can serve these spicy fishcakes as an appetizer with a bowl of sweet chili sauce for everyone to dip into, or add cooked noodles tossed with sesame oil, finely sliced scallions, and soy sauce to make this into a satisfying main course.

SERVES 4 • **READY IN** 20 mins
SPECIAL EQUIPMENT Food processor

- -

1 PURÉE THE INGREDIENTS TO A PASTE

Put the ingredients except the egg, seasoning, and oil in a food processor, and purée to a rough paste, scraping down the sides once or twice. Add the egg and plenty of salt and pepper, and purée again.

2 FLATTEN MIXTURE IN THE PAN

Heat a little of the oil in a large frying pan over medium-high heat. Scoop up 1 tablespoon of the mixture, then carefully slide it into the pan and flatten slightly; it should be about ¾in (2cm) thick. Repeat until all the mixture has been used, but do not crowd the pan (you may need to cook in batches, adding more oil as needed).

3 FRY THE FISHCAKES

Shallow-fry for 1 or 2 minutes on each side until golden, turning carefully. Transfer to a plate lined with paper towels. Serve hot with a drizzle of sweet chili sauce, wedges of fresh lime juice, and arugula leaves.

TIP – You can use pre-prepared and cooked shrimp (fresh or frozen), but make sure that frozen shrimp are thoroughly defrosted first.

Try making miniature versions of these for an easy appetizer. You can make them up to 1 day in advance, storing them in an airtight container in the fridge. Just reheat them in a hot oven until piping hot before serving.

INGREDIENTS

10oz (300g) cooked, peeled, and deveined shrimp

3 garlic cloves, peeled, but left whole

small handful of cilantro leaves

2 hot red chiles, seeded

splash of Thai fish sauce, such as *nam pla*

splash of dark soy sauce

small handful of basil leaves

juice of 2 limes, plus lime wedges to serve

1 egg

salt and freshly ground black pepper

3–4 tbsp vegetable or sunflower oil

sweet chili sauce, to serve

arugula leaves, to serve

INGREDIENTS

½ cup soy sauce

½ cup Chinese rice wine or dry sherry

6 tbsp thinly sliced fresh ginger

4 small sea bass, gutted and rinsed

2 tbsp sesame oil

1 tsp salt

4 scallions, trimmed and thinly sliced

½ cup sunflower oil

4 garlic cloves, chopped

2 small red chiles, seeded and thinly sliced

zest of 2 limes

small handful of chopped cilantro leaves, to serve

5
GARNISH
AND SERVE

CHINESE-STYLE STEAMED BASS

This bright dish is sure to impress your friends with minimal effort. Serve with white basmati rice or Vietnamese glass noodles for a healthy, speedy meal that wouldn't look out of place on a restaurant table.

SERVES 4 • **READY IN** 20 mins

SPECIAL EQUIPMENT Two-tier steamer or large steaming rack

❶ MAKE THE SAUCE

Prepare a two-tier steamer, or position a large steaming rack in a wok with water so it doesn't touch the water. Bring to a boil. Stir together the soy sauce, rice wine, and 4 tbsp ginger, and set aside.

❷ SEASON THE FISH

Using a sharp knife, make slashes in the fish, 1in (2.5cm) apart and not quite as deep as the bone, on both sides. Rub the fish inside and out with the sesame oil and salt.

❸ PREPARE FOR STEAMING

Scatter one-quarter of the scallions over a heatproof serving dish that will hold 2 fish and fit in one of the tiers of the steamer. Place 2 fish on the dish and pour over half the sauce. Repeat with the remaining fish, using a second serving dish. If using a steaming rack, use a heatproof serving dish large enough to hold all 4 fish.

❹ STEAM THE FISH

Place the dishes in the steamer or the large dish on the rack, cover, and steam for 10–12 minutes, or until the fish is cooked through and flakes easily when tested with a knife. Remove the fish, cover, and keep warm.

❺ GARNISH AND SERVE

Meanwhile, heat the sunflower oil in a small saucepan over medium-high heat until shimmering. Scatter the fish with the remaining scallions and ginger, and the garlic, chile, and lime zest. Drizzle the hot oil over the fish and serve with the chopped cilantro.

TIP – To save time, ask your fishmonger to gut the sea bass for you.

ON THE GRILL

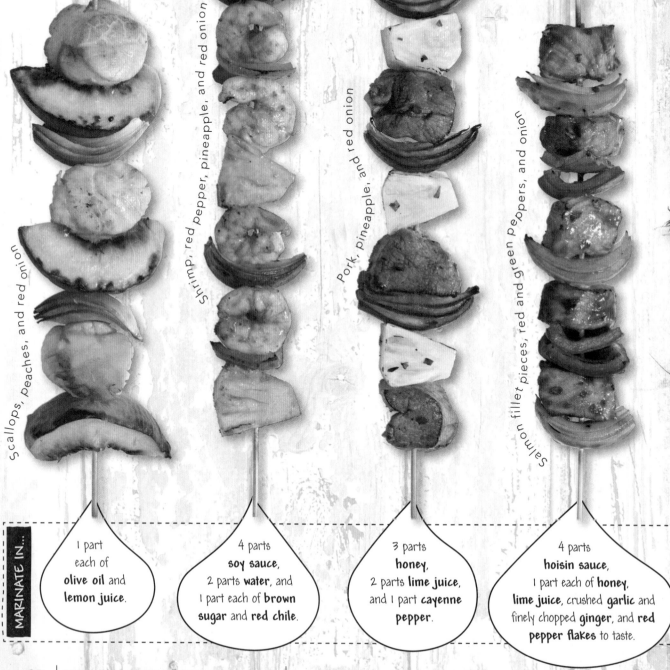

Scallops, peaches, and red onion

Shrimp, red pepper, pineapple, and red onion

Pork, pineapple, and red onion

Salmon fillet pieces, red and green peppers, and onion

MARINATE IN...

1 part each of **olive oil** and **lemon juice**.

4 parts **soy sauce**, 2 parts **water**, and 1 part each of **brown sugar** and **red chile**.

3 parts **honey**, 2 parts **lime juice**, and 1 part **cayenne pepper**.

4 parts **hoisin sauce**, 1 part each of **honey**, **lime juice**, crushed **garlic** and finely chopped **ginger**, and **red pepper flakes** to taste.

Allow these mouthwatering skewers to marinate for 1 hour, if you have time, or simply coat generously and grill immediately. If you're using wooden skewers, soak them in cold water for at least 30 minutes before grilling, to prevent them from burning.

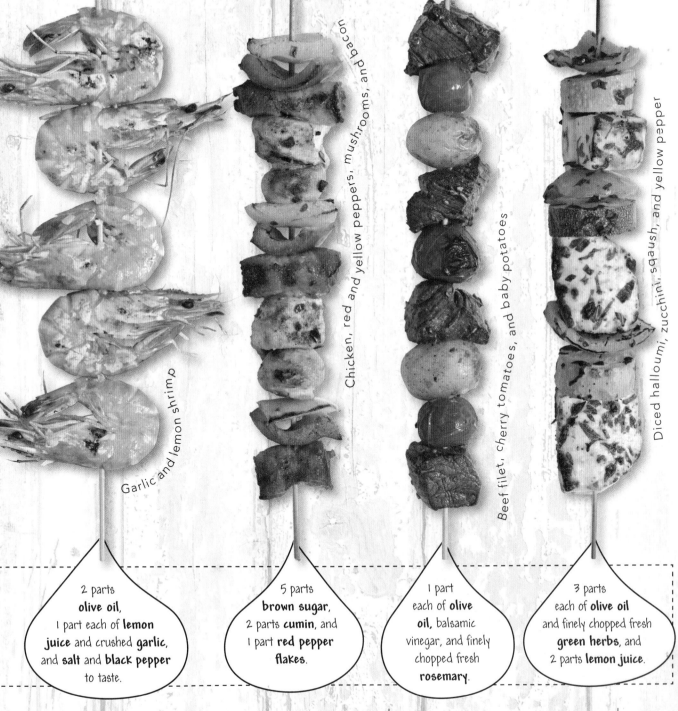

Garlic and lemon shrimp

Chicken, red and yellow peppers, mushrooms, and bacon

Beef filet, cherry tomatoes, and baby potatoes

Diced halloumi, zucchini, squash, and yellow pepper

2 parts **olive oil**, 1 part each of **lemon juice** and crushed **garlic**, and **salt** and **black pepper** to taste.

5 parts **brown sugar**, 2 parts **cumin**, and 1 part **red pepper flakes**.

1 part each of **olive oil**, balsamic vinegar, and finely chopped fresh **rosemary**.

3 parts each of **olive oil** and finely chopped fresh **green herbs**, and 2 parts **lemon juice**.

A MEDLEY OF DIPPING SAUCES

Blend 1 cup **parsley**, ½ cup each of **cilantro** and **oregano**, 5 **garlic cloves**, ¼ cup each of **olive oil**, **mayo**, and **sour cream**, the juice of 1 **lime**, 1 large **avocado**, and a pinch of **red pepper flakes**

Honey mustard

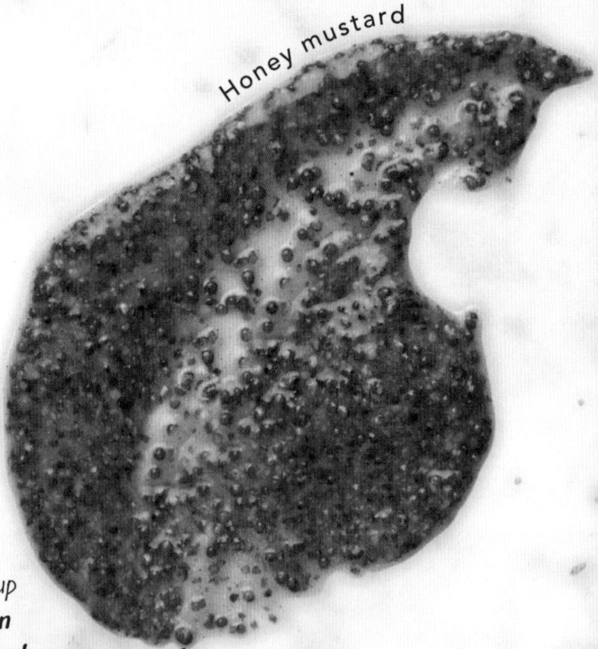

Creamy chimichurri

Combine ⅔ cup **whole-grain mustard**, ¼ cup **honey**, and 2 tbsp **lemon juice**

Combine ⅔ cup **Greek yogurt**, the juice of 2 **lemons**, 2 tbsp **curry powder**, and 2 tsp each of **cayenne pepper** and **garlic powder**

Blend 10oz (300g) **tomatoes**, scant 1oz (25g) mild **green chile pepper**, 3½oz (100g) **red onion**, 2 **garlic cloves**, 1 tsp **red pepper flakes**, 2 tbsp **hot chili sauce**, the juice of 1 **lime**, ½ cup fresh **cilantro**, salt and freshly ground **black pepper**

Tomato salsa dip

Curry yogurt

What better way to serve your skewers (see pp198–9) than with one or more of these dipping sauces? Spicy, sweet, creamy, or tangy, there's something for everyone. Simply combine the ingredients, blending in a food processor where necessary. The quantities here serve 4.

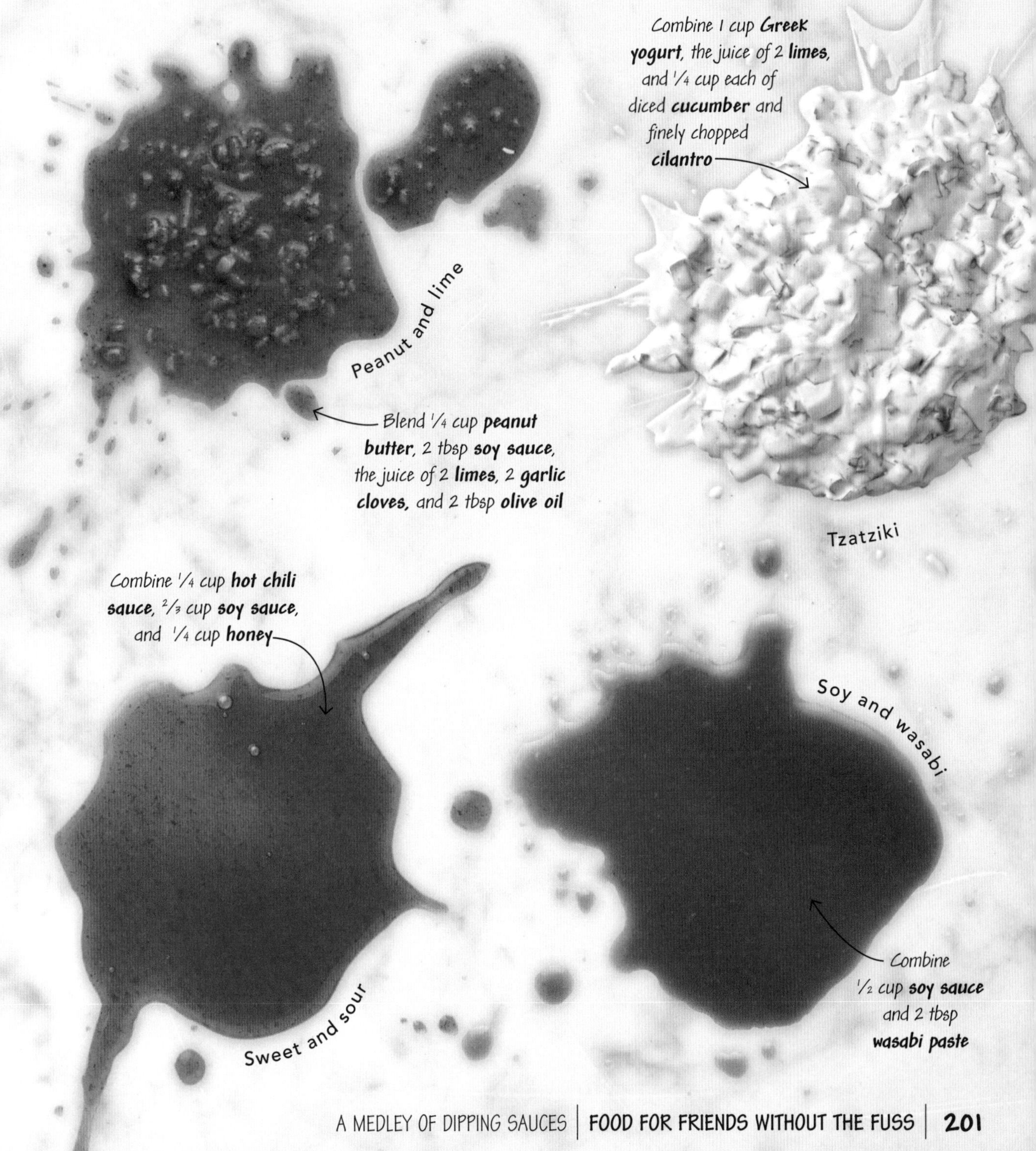

Combine 1 cup **Greek yogurt**, the juice of 2 **limes**, and ¼ cup each of diced **cucumber** and finely chopped **cilantro**

Peanut and lime

Blend ¼ cup **peanut butter**, 2 tbsp **soy sauce**, the juice of 2 **limes**, 2 **garlic cloves**, and 2 tbsp **olive oil**

Tzatziki

Combine ¼ cup **hot chili sauce**, ⅔ cup **soy sauce**, and ¼ cup **honey**

Soy and wasabi

Combine ½ cup **soy sauce** and 2 tbsp **wasabi paste**

Sweet and sour

SEARED DUCK WITH RASPBERRY SAUCE

Seriously impress your guests with this stylish dish, ready in less than half an hour! Tangy raspberry sauce and rich crispy duck are divine together—add wilted, buttery spinach and creamy mashed potatoes to make a more substantial meal.

SERVES 4 • **READY IN** 20 mins

1 SCORE THE SKIN

Use a sharp knife to score the skin on the duck breasts. Rub the meat generously with salt and pepper.

2 COOK THE DUCK BREASTS

Place the duck skin-side down in a heavy-bottomed frying pan over medium-low heat. Allow the duck fat to render (melt) for 10–12 minutes. Turn and cook for another 3–5 minutes on the other side. Set aside to rest. Keep warm.

3 MAKE THE SAUCE

While the duck is cooking, melt the butter in a separate pan. Add the sugar and shallots and cook until caramelized. Press the raspberries through a strainer to make a smooth sauce. Add the raspberry pulp, cardamom, and vinegar to the pan. Cook, stirring frequently, for 5–7 minutes.

4 PLATE UP AND SERVE

Transfer the duck to a serving plate and serve topped with the raspberry sauce.

TIP – To prepare the cardamom, split the pods open with a knife point and scrape the seeds out. Discard the pods and crush the seeds into a powder using a mortar and pestle or, if you don't have one, using the end of a rolling pin and a sturdy mixing bowl.

1 SCORE SKIN → **2** COOK DUCK → **3** MAKE SAUCE → **4** PLATE UP AND SERVE

INGREDIENTS

1lb 5oz (600g) skin-on duck breasts

salt and freshly ground black pepper

FOR THE SAUCE
1 tbsp butter

1 tbsp brown sugar

3½oz (100g) shallots, finely chopped

7oz (200g) fresh raspberries, seeded and roughly chopped

4 cardamom pods, seeds removed and crushed

1 tbsp red wine vinegar

PORK CHOPS WITH FRIED APPLES

This dish allows you to feed your guests in style just minutes after they arrive. The sweet, caramelized apples provide a quick and tasty accompaniment to the salty pork, and the creamed spinach adds a flash of iron-rich greenery.

SERVES 4 • **READY IN** 20 mins

1 COOK THE PORK

Season the pork well with salt, pepper, and red pepper flakes. Heat 1 tablespoon of the oil in a large frying pan and cook the pork for 3–5 minutes on each side, depending on thickness, until cooked through. Set it aside, loosely covered with foil to keep warm while it rests.

2 PREPARE THE APPLES

Add the remaining 1 tablespoon of oil and the butter to the pan and allow it to bubble up. Add the apple pieces, pour in the lemon juice, sprinkle with the sugar, and season with salt and pepper.

3 CARAMELIZE THE APPLES

Cook the apples over medium heat for 5–7 minutes, turning occasionally, until they soften and start to caramelize. Turn them gently using 2 spatulas, so the pieces don't break up.

4 WILT THE SPINACH

Meanwhile, make the creamed spinach. Melt the butter and oil in a separate large, deep-sided frying pan. Cook the garlic for 1 minute, then add the baby spinach. Turn it through the oil and sauté it for 2–3 minutes, until cooked through. Add the cream, season well, bring to a boil, and reduce. Serve alongside the pork chops, each one topped with one-quarter of the apples.

INGREDIENTS

4 x 3½oz (100g) boneless pork chops

salt and freshly ground black pepper

1 tsp red pepper flakes

2 tbsp olive oil

1 tbsp butter

4 small apples, peeled, cored, and quartered

1 tbsp lemon juice

½ tsp light brown sugar

FOR THE CREAMED SPINACH
1 tbsp butter
1 tbsp olive oil
1 small garlic clove, crushed
14oz (400g) baby spinach leaves
½ cup heavy cream
salt and freshly ground black pepper

HARISSA-SPICED LAMB CHOPS

Spice up some lamb chops with Moroccan-inspired seasoning, add mashed chickpeas and chopped tomatoes tossed with olive oil and balsamic vinegar, and you've got a tasty feast on the table in less than half an hour.

SERVES 4 • **READY IN** 20 mins

1 BROIL THE CHOPS

Preheat the broiler to its medium setting. Place the chops on a foil-lined baking sheet and broil on one side for 8 minutes.

2 MAKE THE RUB

While the chops are broiling, place the bread crumbs, zest, harissa, cilantro, and olive oil in a bowl, season with salt and pepper, and stir well to combine evenly.

3 SEASON THE CHOPS

Turn the chops when ready, and press the bread crumb and harissa mixture onto the uncooked side of each chop. Broil for another 8 minutes.

4 COOK THE CHICKPEAS

Meanwhile, make the chickpea mash. Heat the oil in a saucepan over medium heat, add the onion, and cook for 5 minutes. Add the garlic and cook for 2 minutes. Stir in the chickpeas, lemon juice, and extra virgin olive oil, and gently heat.

5 MAKE THE MASH

Remove from the heat and mash roughly with a potato masher; it should not be smooth. Stir in the cilantro and season generously. Serve the chops with the chickpea mash and a dressed tomato salad.

TIP – Make the bread crumb topping up to 3 days ahead, cover, and store in an airtight container in the fridge.

INGREDIENTS

8 x 3½oz (100g) lamb loin chops

1 cup fresh white bread crumbs

finely grated zest of 1 lemon

1 tbsp harissa paste

2 tbsp finely chopped cilantro leaves

2 tsp olive oil

salt and freshly ground black pepper

FOR THE CHICKPEA MASH

1 tbsp olive oil

1 red onion, finely chopped

2 garlic cloves, finely chopped

2 x 14oz (400g) cans chickpeas, drained and rinsed

1½ tbsp lemon juice

2 tbsp extra virgin olive oil

2 tbsp finely chopped cilantro leaves

tomato salad, to serve

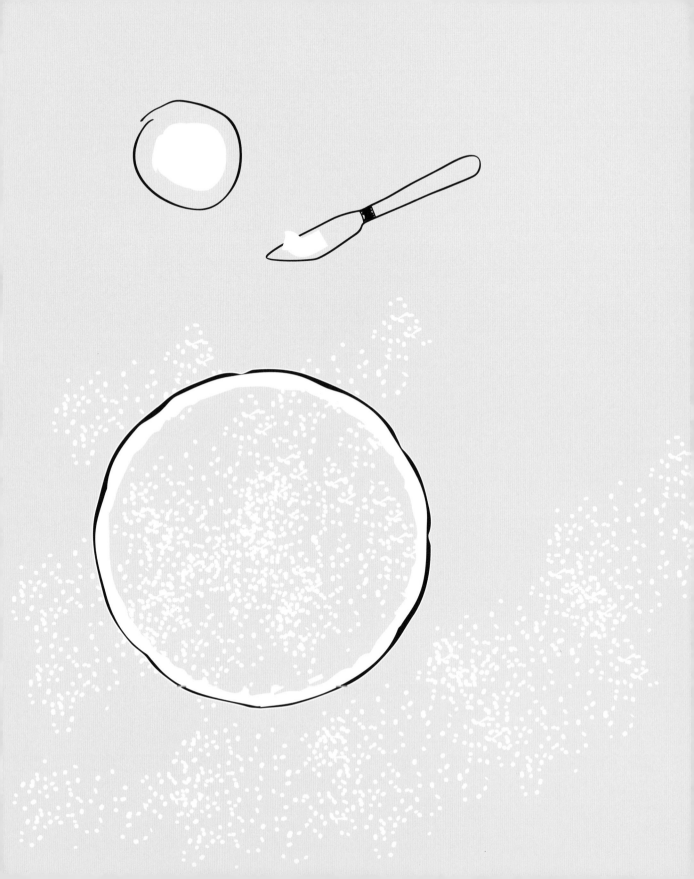

SHORT AND SWEET

FRESH ORANGES WITH CARAMEL AND PASSION FRUIT

Add homemade caramel and zingy passion fruit to your oranges to lift this fruit-bowl staple to a whole new level! Throw in fresh mint leaves and chopped pistachios, and serve with Greek yogurt for a colorful, refreshing dessert.

SERVES 4 • **READY IN** 15 mins

- -

1 MAKE THE CARAMEL

Put the sugar in a saucepan with 2 tablespoons of cold water. Stir, then heat gently without stirring, until the sugar melts. Boil rapidly until the sugar syrup turns a rich golden brown. Remove from the heat and add 2 tablespoons of water. Stir over low heat until the caramel dissolves, then let cool.

2 PREPARE THE ORANGES

Slice off the top and bottom from each orange and place on a cutting board. Carefully slice off the skin and pith, leaving as much flesh as possible, and following the sides of the orange so you keep the shape of the fruit. Slice the oranges horizontally into thin strips, discarding any seeds as you come across them. Arrange the orange slices on a serving platter. Pour over any remaining juice.

3 DRIZZLE AND DECORATE

Drizzle the caramel over the orange slices and sprinkle with the cinnamon. Slice the passion fruit in half, scoop out the seeds, and scatter with the pistachios, if using. Decorate with the mint leaves and serve.

PLAN OF ACTION!

1 MAKE CARAMEL → 2 PREPARE ORANGES → 3 DRIZZLE AND DECORATE

INGREDIENTS

¼ cup granulated sugar

4 oranges

good pinch of ground cinnamon

seeds from 2 passion fruit

small handful of chopped pistachios (optional)

handful of mint leaves, to decorate

MIXED BERRIES WITH WHITE CHOCOLATE SAUCE

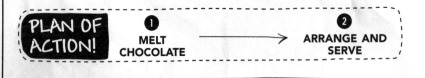

10 MINS OR LESS!

A refreshing and luxurious recipe, this dessert pairs a warm and rich sauce with sweet, frozen fruit—a great way to use up that package of berries in the freezer!

SERVES 4 • **READY IN** 10 mins

INGREDIENTS

- 4½oz (125g) good-quality white chocolate, plus extra to serve (optional)
- ⅔ cup heavy cream or whipping cream
- 1lb (450g) package frozen mixed berries, such as raspberries, strawberries, and blackberries

① MELT THE CHOCOLATE
Break the chocolate into pieces and place in a saucepan over low heat. Add the cream and bring almost to a boil, stirring constantly, until the chocolate has melted and the mixture is well combined.

② ARRANGE AND SERVE
Divide the berries among 4 serving dishes. Pour the chocolate mixture over the top and serve topped with grated white chocolate, if you like.

PLAN OF ACTION!

① MELT CHOCOLATE ⟶ ② ARRANGE AND SERVE

LYCHEES WITH GINGER AND STAR ANISE

The subtle and fragrant aniseed flavor of the star anise goes well with the refreshing lychees and ginger in this quick and cooling dessert.

SERVES 4 • **READY IN** 10 mins, plus marinating

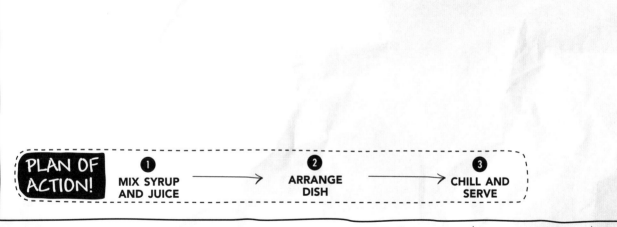

INGREDIENTS

- 2 tbsp ginger syrup
- 1 x 14oz (400ml) can lychees, drained and 2 tsp juice reserved
- 1 star anise
- 2 pieces candied ginger, finely diced
- Greek yogurt, to serve

1 MIX THE SYRUP AND JUICE

Place the ginger syrup and reserved lychee juice in a small bowl and mix well to combine.

2 ARRANGE THE DISH

Place the lychees and star anise in a glass serving dish. Scatter with the ginger and drizzle with the ginger syrup and lychee juice mixture.

3 CHILL AND SERVE

Chill in the fridge for 30 minutes, or longer if you have the time, for the flavors to develop. Divide between serving glasses and serve topped with Greek yogurt.

PLAN OF ACTION!

1 MIX SYRUP AND JUICE → 2 ARRANGE DISH → 3 CHILL AND SERVE

WARM FRUIT COMPÔTE

This dish is ideal for fall and winter, when supplies of fresh fruit are limited; it's a sweet, spiced dessert that's sure to warm you up on a cold day. Serve with yogurt on the side and honey drizzled over, if you like.

MAKES 10 • **READY IN** 15–20 mins

1 STEW THE FRUIT

Melt the butter in a heavy saucepan over medium heat. Add the fruit and cinnamon stick. Cook gently, stirring often, until the fruit has completely softened.

2 STIR IN THE SUGAR

Stir in the sugar and heat for another couple of minutes, or until the sugar has dissolved.

3 SPRINKLE WITH LEMON JUICE AND SERVE

Remove the pan from the heat, sprinkle with lemon juice, and serve warm with a spoonful of yogurt and a drizzle of honey.

TIP – The compôte can be made up to 3 days in advance, covered, and refrigerated.

For convenience, keep a bag of frozen cherries in the freezer and use instead of the fresh fruit in the compôte. It will cut down the preparation time. Any leftover compôte is delicious with granola (see pp30–33).

PLAN OF ACTION!

1. **STEW FRUIT** → 2. **STIR IN SUGAR** → 3. **SPRINKLE WITH LEMON JUICE**

INGREDIENTS

2 tbsp butter

6 dried prunes, chopped

6 dried apricots, chopped

2 large apples, peeled, cored, and chopped

1 firm pear, peeled, cored, and chopped

1 cinnamon stick

2 tsp sugar

2 tsp lemon juice

yogurt and honey, to serve

ORANGE SORBET

Often served in restaurants as a refreshing palate cleanser between courses, sorbets also make lovely, light summer desserts.

SERVES 2 • **READY IN** 20 mins, plus cooling and freezing

SPECIAL EQUIPMENT Hand-held electric blender

- ⅔ cup granulated sugar
- 2 large oranges
- 1 tbsp orange-flower water
- 1 egg white

MAKE THE SYRUP

1 DISSOLVE

orange zest

VEGETABLE PEELER

sugar

WOODEN SPOON

SAUCEPAN

Dissolve the sugar in 1¼ cups of water over low heat. Add the zest from the oranges and simmer for 10 minutes.

2 MIX

JUICER

orange juice

orange-flower water

Remove from the heat, let cool slightly, then stir in the juice from the oranges and the orange-flower water.

3 STRAIN

SIEVE

PREPARE THE EGG WHITE

WHILE THE SYRUP IS COOLING, PREPARE THE EGG WHITE.

4 WHISK

ELECTRIC BLENDER

SHALLOW CONTAINER

Strain the syrup, discarding the zest, and let cool completely.

Place the egg white in a bowl and whisk until soft peaks form.

COMBINE AND FREEZE

5 FOLD

SPATULA

FREEZERPROOF CONTAINER

Transfer the syrup to a freezerproof container and fold in the whisked egg white. Freeze for 4 hours, or until solid.

6 MASH

FORK

Mash with a fork to break up any ice crystals, then freeze again. To serve, let soften for 10–15 minutes.

INGREDIENTS

4 ripe bananas

1 tsp
vanilla extract

PLAN OF ACTION!

1 PEEL AND FREEZE → **2** BLEND IT UP → **3** EAT OR REFREEZE

QUICK BANANA ICE CREAM

This is the quickest and easiest ice cream you will ever make—and it's super healthy, too! This dessert is a great way to use up any ripening bananas in your fruit bowl, and you don't even need an ice-cream maker.

SERVES 4 • **READY IN** 5 mins, plus freezing
SPECIAL EQUIPMENT Food processor

1 PEEL AND FREEZE

Simply peel the bananas, chop them into ¾in (2cm) chunks, and place them in a freezer container. Seal and put in the freezer until frozen.

2 BLEND IT UP

When the bananas are frozen solid, process them in a food processor with the vanilla extract, until you have a smooth, thick ice cream. You may need to scrape down the sides a couple of times during the process.

3 EAT NOW OR REFREEZE

Either eat the softened banana ice cream immediately, or freeze for a few minutes for it to firm up once more before serving.

TIP – If you have ripening bananas that you can't use up quickly enough, peel them, cut into chunks, and freeze on a plate. When they are frozen solid, transfer to a freezer bag and add more bananas until you have enough to make this ice cream.

A few spoonfuls of chocolate and hazelnut spread, or smooth peanut butter, added to the food processor along with the bananas works well here, too.

A MONTH OF SUNDAES

For the spice mix, combine 1 tbsp **ground cinnamon**, 2 tsp **ground ginger**, and ½ tsp each of **ground nutmeg**, crushed **cardamom seeds**, and **ground cloves**.

CHOCOLATE BROWNIE AND STRAWBERRIES

Chocolate brownie pieces, chocolate ice cream, halved strawberries, and whipped cream.

BANANA AND TOFFEE

Banana muffin or banana bread, vanilla ice cream, banana slices, and **toffee sauce**.

CHOCOLATE AND PEANUT BUTTER PRETZEL

Chopped **pretzels**, vanilla ice cream, melted **peanut butter**, and chocolate sauce.

PUMPKIN PIE-SPICED BLONDIE

Blondie brownie, vanilla ice cream, crumbled graham crackers, and pumpkin pie spice.

A sundae is the ideal speedy, decadent dessert—simply throw together a few key ingredients with some ice cream, drizzle with sauce or syrup, and serve in a beautiful glass to show off the layers! They are also a great way to turn brownies (see pp242-5) into an indulgent dessert.

Toss the **pineapple pieces** in **dark brown sugar**. Grill for 7–10 minutes or until bubbling.

Toast the **coconut shreds** in a dry frying pan until they begin to brown at the edges.

You can substitute **toasted marshmallows** for the marshmallow fluff.

COCONUT AND GRILLED PINEAPPLE

Toasted **coconut shreds**, coconut ice cream, grilled **pineapple pieces**, **chocolate sauce**, and whipped cream.

GINGER SNAP AND PECAN

Crushed **ginger snaps**, **dulce de leche ice cream**, and **caramel sauce**.

MARSHMALLOW AND BANANA SPLIT

Vanilla ice cream, sliced **banana**, **marshmallow fluff**, and chocolate sauce.

GINGER AND DARK CHOCOLATE

Dark chocolate pieces, vanilla ice cream, candied ginger pieces, and crushed **walnuts**.

SHAKES AND FLOATS

GINGERBREAD SHAKE
Blend 2 scoops of vanilla ice cream, 2 cups milk,
1 tsp ground cinnamon, 1 tsp grated nutmeg,
1 tsp vanilla extract, and 2 tsp ground ginger.
Garnish with crushed ginger snaps.

GRASSHOPPER SHAKE
Blend 2 scoops of mint chocolate chip
ice cream, 1 tsp mint extract, 1 cup
milk, and 1 cup chocolate milk.
Garnish with peppermint
patties and fresh mint leaves.

BANANA AND
PEANUT BUTTER SHAKE
Blend 2 cups milk, 2 scoops of Quick
Banana Ice Cream (see pp218–19), and
½ cup smooth peanut butter. Garnish
with dried banana chips.

FROZEN STRAWBERRY SHAKE
Blend 1 cup milk, 1 cup frozen
strawberry yogurt, and 3½oz
(100g) fresh strawberries, hulled.
Garnish with slices of fresh strawberry.

A milkshake or float makes for a delicious, drinkable dessert that can be ready in a couple of minutes. For the shakes, use your preferred milk and combine the ingredients in a blender. For the floats, pour in the fizzy drink first, let it settle, then pop in a scoop or two of ice cream or sorbet. These quantities make 2 tall glasses.

LEMONADE FLOAT

Divide ⅔ cup traditional lemonade and 1½ cups lemon-and-lime soda between two glasses. Drop a scoop of lemon sorbet into each glass.

BERRY AND GINGER ALE FLOAT

Divide 2 cups ginger ale between two glasses. Drop a scoop each of blackberry sorbet and raspberry sorbet into each glass.

FLOATS

NEAPOLITAN FLOAT

Divide 2 cups soda water between two glasses. Drop a small scoop each of strawberry, chocolate, and vanilla ice cream into each glass. Drizzle strawberry sauce and chocolate sauce over each float.

CHERRY COLA FLOAT

Divide 2 cups cherry cola between two glasses. Drop a scoop each of chocolate ice cream and cherry ice cream into each glass. Drizzle chocolate sauce over each float.

INGREDIENTS

2 cups
heavy cream

1 tsp vanilla extract

2 tbsp superfine sugar

5½oz (150g) store-bought
meringues

10oz (300g) strawberries,
finely chopped

5½oz (150g)
raspberries

FOR THE FRUIT COULIS
10oz (150g) strawberries
10oz (150g) raspberries
¼ cup superfine sugar

ETON MESS WITH WARM FRUIT COULIS

10 MINS OR LESS!

This is a crowd-pleasing, summery dessert that's very quick to make. Serve in sundae glasses or clean glass jars to show off the pretty pink and white layers. For a lighter taste, try replacing the heavy cream with Greek yogurt.

SERVES 6 • **READY IN** 10 mins, plus chilling

1 WHISK THE CREAM

Whisk the cream until it is very stiff, then whisk in the vanilla extract and fold in the sugar.

2 SMASH THE MERINGUES

Place the meringues in a freezer bag and smash with a rolling pin to break into uneven pebble-sized pieces. It's nice to have a mixture of large pieces and smaller crumbs, for the best texture.

3 COMBINE THE MIXTURE

Fold together the cream mixture, the meringues, and the fruit. Cover and chill while you make the coulis.

4 MAKE THE COULIS

Put the fruit for the coulis, sugar, and 3 tablespoons of water into a small saucepan with a lid. Cover, place over medium heat, and bring to a boil, then remove the lid, stir, and simmer the fruit for about 5 minutes, or until it is soft.

5 BLEND AND SERVE

Blend the fruit with a hand-held blender until smooth, then press it through a nylon strainer to remove all the seeds. Pour over the Eton mess while still warm.

For a tropical twist, substitute a peeled and sliced mango for the strawberries and raspberries, then use the flesh and seeds of a passion fruit to replace the coulis.

RASPBERRY CHEESECAKE

This fresh and light cheesecake requires no cooking and takes very little time to prepare. You can make it up to 24 hours ahead and chill until required.

SERVES 6 • **READY IN** 15 mins, plus chilling
SPECIAL EQUIPMENT 8in (20cm) round springform pan

- 4 tbsp unsalted butter
- 3¹⁄₂oz (100g) dark chocolate, broken into pieces
- 5¹⁄₂oz (150g) graham crackers
- 14oz (400g) mascarpone cheese
- grated zest and juice of 2 limes, plus extra zest for garnishing
- 2–3 tbsp confectioner's sugar, plus extra for dusting
- 8oz (225g) strawberries

MAKE THE CRUST

1 MELT

dark chocolate

butter

SAUCEPAN

Melt the butter and chocolate together over low heat.

2 CRUSH

PLASTIC BAG

ROLLING PIN

graham crackers

Seal the graham crackers in a plastic bag and crush with a rolling pin.

3 COMBINE

TRANSFER THE MIXTURE TO A SPRING-FORM PAN.

WOODEN SPOON

Add the crushed crackers to the chocolate and butter and stir well to combine.

4 FORM

SPRINGFORM PAN

Spread the graham cracker mixture out evenly, pressing it down firmly into the bottom and sides of the pan.

5 BEAT

lime zest and juice

confectioner's sugar

mascarpone cheese

Place the mascarpone cheese, lime zest (reserving some for garnishing), and lime juice in a bowl and beat to combine. Then add the confectioner's sugar and mix well.

ASSEMBLE THE CAKE

6 SPREAD

Pour the cheese mixture over the cracker base.

SPATULA

Spread the mixture out evenly and smooth over the top with a spatula. Chill in the fridge for 1 hour.

7 ARRANGE AND SERVE

Arrange the raspberries over the cheesecake, dust with confectioner's sugar, and garnish with lime zest.

INGREDIENTS

¾ cup superfine sugar

⅔ cup light corn syrup

1 cup
shelled pistachios

2 tbsp butter, cut into
cubes, plus extra
for greasing

1 tsp baking soda

1 tsp vanilla extract

PLAN OF ACTION!

1 HEAT SUGAR → 2 ADD PISTACHIOS → 3 STIR IN DRY INGREDIENTS

4

→ COOL
AND SMASH

PISTACHIO BRITTLE

Brittles are a simple, fun sweet that can be made quickly from pantry ingredients. You can dig into this cracked straight from the pan, or store it in an airtight container and keep it for a few days.

SERVES 6–8 • **READY IN** 20 mins, plus cooling
SPECIAL EQUIPMENT Sugar thermometer (see also "TIP," below)

❶ HEAT THE SUGAR AND WATER

In a heavy-bottomed saucepan, combine the sugar, corn syrup, and ¼ cup water over medium heat. Cook, stirring frequently with a wooden spoon, until a sugar thermometer dipped into the liquid reads 325°F (160°C) and the sugar turns brittle and golden brown.

❷ ADD THE PISTACHIOS

At this stage, known as "hard breaking point," add the pistachios. Continue stirring until the temperature rises to 325°F (160°C) again.

❸ STIR IN THE REMAINING INGREDIENTS

Remove from the heat and stir in the butter, baking soda, and vanilla extract. Continue to stir as it foams and the butter melts.

❹ POUR, COOL, AND SMASH

Pour onto a greased 9 x 14in (23 x 35cm) baking sheet and let it cool completely. Break into pieces and store in an airtight container.

TIP – If you do not have a sugar thermometer, drop a small amount of the mixture into a glass of cold water— if it turns brittle and snaps, the mixture is hot enough.

Why not
try combining different dried fruit and nuts to find your favorite combination? Peanuts are a classic and delicious addition.

PANNA COTTA

This simple Italian dessert is easy to prepare and makes a refreshing end to a meal, especially served with a fruit compôte (see p214) or a summery fruit coulis (see "tip," below).

SERVES 4 • **READY IN** 15 mins, plus setting
SPECIAL EQUIPMENT 4 x 5fl oz (150ml) ramekins

INGREDIENTS

- 1¾ cup half-and-half
- 1 cup whole milk
- ½ cup superfine sugar
- 4 sheets of gelatin
- 1 tbsp sunflower oil
- fruit compôte, fruit coulis, or fruit salad, to serve
- crushed pistachio nuts, to serve

❶ HEAT THE CREAM AND MILK

Heat the cream and milk in a saucepan. When it is hot, but not boiling, pour it into a bowl and whisk in the sugar until dissolved.

❷ SOAK THE GELATIN

Meanwhile, soak the gelatin in a bowl of water for 5 minutes, squeeze out the excess, and add to the hot cream. Heat it very gently, stirring, until the gelatin dissolves.

❸ PREPARE AND FILL THE RAMEKINS

Rub the insides of four 5fl oz (150ml) ramekins with a piece of paper towel dipped in the oil. Divide the cream mixture between the ramekins, cover, and cool. Transfer to the fridge for at least 2 hours, or until the cream has set.

❹ TURN OUT AND GARNISH

To serve, fill a bowl with hot water and carefully dip the base of each ramekin into the water. Run a small knife around the edge of each ramekin, and turn the panna cottas onto plates. Garnish with fruit compôte, fruit coulis, or a fruit salad, and a sprinkling of crushed pistachios.

TIP – You can make a fruit coulis while the panna cotta is setting. Put 3 tbsp of maple syrup, 3 tbsp of orange juice, and 8oz (225g) of halved strawberries in a pan, and simmer gently for 5 minutes. Remove from the heat and purée in a food processor or blender until smooth, or spoon through a sieve.

PLAN OF ACTION! ❶ **HEAT MILK AND CREAM** → ❷ **SOAK GELATIN** → ❸ **PREPARE AND FILL RAMEKINS** → ❹ **TURN OUT AND GARNISH**

CARAMELIZED APPLE AND CHOCOLATE CRÊPES

Indulge in some paper-thin, French-style crêpes for an easy and delicious dessert. Make sure you use crisp apples, as these will keep their substance and texture better during cooking.

MAKES 4–6 • **READY IN** 20 mins, plus resting (optional)

INGREDIENTS

- ¼ cup all-purpose flour
- salt
- 1 egg, lightly beaten
- ⅔ cup milk
- ½ cup heavy cream
- pat of butter
- 2–3 tbsp granulated sugar, depending on the sweetness of the apples
- 4 pink-skinned apples, sliced
- vegetable oil
- 4½oz (125g) dark chocolate, grated

❶ MAKE THE BATTER

Sift the flour into a mixing bowl with a pinch of salt and make a well in the center. Put the egg and a little of the milk in the well. Using a wooden spoon, gradually stir the egg mixture, letting a little of the flour fall in as you go and adding the rest of the milk a little at a time. When it is all incorporated, whisk the mixture with a balloon whisk to remove any lumps. Transfer to the fridge to rest for 15 minutes, if you have time.

❷ WHIP THE CREAM

Meanwhile, put the cream in a mixing bowl and whisk until lightly whipped, then set to one side.

❸ CARAMELIZE THE APPLES

Put the butter and sugar in a frying pan over low heat and stir until the sugar has dissolved. Add the apple slices and toss well. Cook for 5–10 minutes, or until caramelized, then put to one side and keep warm.

❹ COOK THE CRÊPES

While the apples are caramelizing, cook the crêpes. Heat a pancake pan or small frying pan over high heat. When hot, add a tiny amount of vegetable oil, then swirl it around the pan and pour it into a bowl. Add 2 tablespoons of batter to the pan and swirl it around so it covers the base. Loosen the edges of the crêpe with a palette knife and cook for 1 minute, or until golden. Flip the crêpe and cook the other side for a minute or so. Slide onto a warmed plate and repeat until all the mixture has been used.

❺ FILL, FOLD, AND SERVE

To serve, pile some of the apple mixture and a dollop of cream onto each crêpe, fold, and top with plenty of chocolate shavings.

PLAN OF ACTION! ❶ MAKE BATTER → ❷ WHIP CREAM → ❸ CARAMELIZE APPLES → ❹ COOK CRÊPES → ❺ FILL, FOLD, AND SERVE

CINNAMON CHURROS

These cinnamon- and sugar-sprinkled Spanish snacks are quick to make and will be devoured just as quickly! Try dipping them in this spicy chocolate sauce.

MAKES 20 • **READY IN** 20 mins, plus cooling
SPECIAL EQUIPMENT Piping bag • ¾in (2cm) star-shaped nozzle

- -

- 2 tbsp unsalted butter
- 1¼ cups all-purpose flour
- ¼ cup granulated sugar
- 1 tsp baking powder
- 3½ cups peanut or sunflower oil
- 1 tsp ground cinnamon

- 1 tbsp granulated sugar
- 1 tbsp unsalted butter
- pinch of salt
- ¼ tsp chile powder or cayenne pepper, to taste

FOR THE CHOCOLATE CHILE SAUCE

- 1¾oz (50g) good-quality dark chocolate, broken into pieces
- ⅔ cup heavy cream

MAKE THE BATTER

2 STIR

Mix the butter with ½ cup of boiling water.

HEAT-RESISTANT JUG
butter

1 COMBINE

SIEVE
baking powder
flour
sugar

Sift together the flour and baking powder into a bowl, and add half the sugar.

3 MIX

Beat the hot butter liquid and flour mixture together to form a thick paste.

WOODEN SPOON

PIPE AND FRY THE CHURROS

WHILE THE BATTER IS COOLING, HEAT THE OIL FOR DEEP-FRYING.

4 HEAT

oil

Pour the oil to a depth of 4in (10cm).

cube of bread

Heat the oil to 375°F (190°C). When it's hot enough, a cube of bread popped into the pan will turn golden brown in 1 minute.

5 PIPE

PIPING BAG

Meanwhile, spoon the cooled batter into a piping bag fitted with a star-shaped nozzle.

6 FRY AND DRAIN

SLOTTED SPOON

PAPER TOWELS

Pipe 2¾in (7cm) lengths of the batter directly into the hot oil. Cook the churros in batches for 1–2 minutes on each side before letting them drain.

7 TOSS

sugar and cinnamon

PLATE

Toss the hot churros in the remaining sugar and the cinnamon.

8 MELT

heavy cream

chocolate

sugar

chile powder

butter

HEATPROOF BOWL

SAUCEPAN

Make sure the bowl doesn't touch the water when you're making the sauce, otherwise it will become too hot and may burn and spoil.

MAKE THE SAUCE

Heat the sauce ingredients in a medium, heatproof bowl over a saucepan of barely simmering water. Stir constantly for 3–4 minutes until the sauce melds together.

FRESH FRUIT HAND PIES

HOW TO MAKE

MAKES 12-14

- 3½ cups all-purpose flour, plus extra for dusting
- 16 tbsp butter, chilled and diced
- ⅓ cup brown sugar
- pinch of salt

Place all the ingredients in a food processor, add ¼ cup of water, and process until a smooth dough forms. Cover with plastic wrap and chill for 1 hour.

To form the pies, roll out the dough on a floured surface. Use a cookie cutter or tumbler to cut 3-4in (7.5-10cm) wide circles. Place 1 tbsp of the filling on one half of each circle and fold over the other half to create a half-moon shape. Place on lined baking sheets and bake for 15-17 minutes at 350°F (180°C), or until golden brown.

7oz (200g) diced **pineapple**, 7oz (200g) diced **mango**, juice of 2 **limes**, and 1 tbsp **brown sugar**.

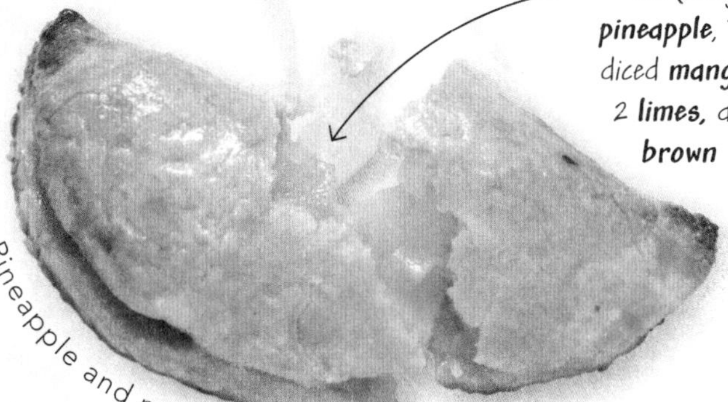

Pineapple and mango

2 **peaches**, pitted and chopped into bite-sized pieces, and 1 tbsp **ground ginger**.

Peach and ginger

18-20 **strawberries**, sliced and tossed with 3 tbsp **honey**.

Strawberries and honey

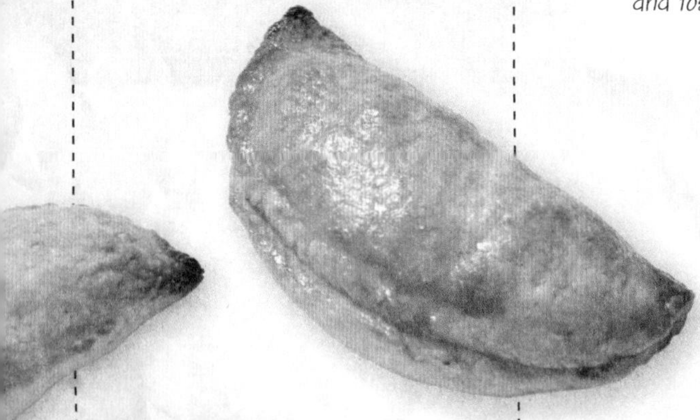

These neat little pies are a treat at any time of the day and make for the perfect portable snack. Try these delicious fillings or experiment with your own favorite fruity combinations. You could even freeze a batch of the dough and keep it ready for when inspiration strikes!

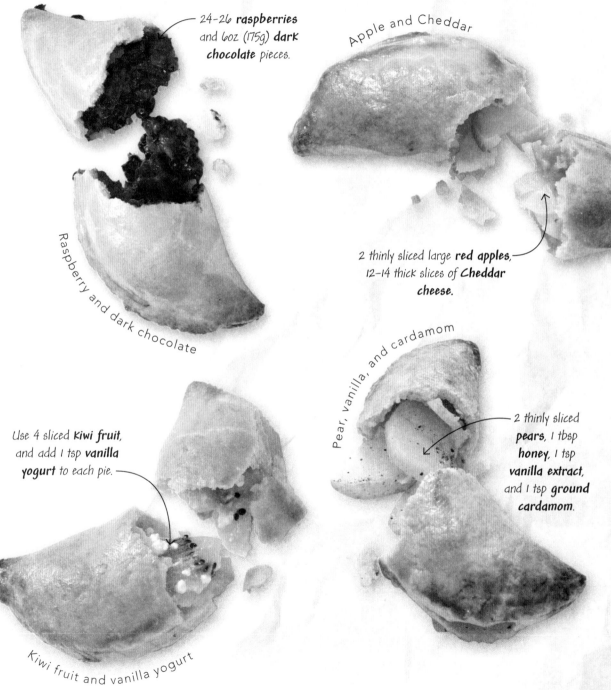

24-26 **raspberries** and 6oz (175g) **dark chocolate** pieces.

Apple and Cheddar

Raspberry and dark chocolate

2 thinly sliced large **red apples**, 12-14 thick slices of **Cheddar cheese**.

Pear, vanilla, and cardamom

Use 4 sliced **kiwi fruit**, and add 1 tsp **vanilla yogurt** to each pie.

2 thinly sliced **pears**, 1 tbsp **honey**, 1 tsp **vanilla extract**, and 1 tsp **ground cardamom**.

Kiwi fruit and vanilla yogurt

FRESH FRUIT HAND PIES | SHORT AND SWEET | 235

EASY BANOFFEE PIE

Using a store-bought tart crust is a sneaky way of creating an impressive dessert without having to make your own pastry. You can have a perfect banoffee pie on the table in just 15 minutes!

SERVES 8 • **READY IN** 15 mins
SPECIAL EQUIPMENT Electric hand mixer

INGREDIENTS

- 8in (20cm) store-bought tart crust
- 7oz (200g) store-bought thick caramel sauce (such as dulce de leche)
- 2–3 ripe bananas
- 1¼ cups heavy cream
- scant 1oz (25g) dark chocolate

1 FILL THE TART CRUST

Place the tart crust on a serving plate. Spoon in the caramel sauce and spread evenly over the bottom. Slice the bananas and scatter over the top.

2 WHIP THE CREAM

Put the cream in a bowl and beat with an electric hand mixer until soft peaks form. Spoon the cream over the bananas.

3 ADD CHOCOLATE AND SERVE

Grate the chocolate evenly over the top and serve.

Why not try different fillings for the tart crust? Whipped cream or pastry cream topped with raspberries or sliced strawberries is delicious.

PLAN OF ACTION!

1 FILL TART CRUST → **2** WHIP CREAM → **3** ADD CHOCOLATE AND SERVE

NO-BAKE CHOCOLATE CAKE

Also known as a chocolate fridge cake, this no-bake treat is perfect as a lunchbox snack. Vary the fruit and nuts to your liking—chopped cherries and hazelnuts work well, for example.

SERVES 6 • **READY IN** 10 mins, plus chilling
SPECIAL EQUIPMENT 8in (20cm) square baking pan

INGREDIENTS

- 11 tbsp butter, plus extra for greasing
- 9oz (250g) dark chocolate, broken into pieces
- 2 tbsp agave syrup
- 1lb (450g) graham crackers, crushed
- handful of plump golden raisins
- handful of unskinned almonds, roughly chopped

❶ MELT THE CHOCOLATE MIXTURE

Lightly grease the pan. In a large saucepan, combine the butter, chocolate, and syrup. Cook over low heat, stirring, until melted and smooth. Remove from the heat.

❷ ADD THE DRY INGREDIENTS

Stir the graham crackers, raisins, and almonds into the chocolate mixture. Mix well, then press the mixture into the pan with the back of a spoon.

❸ CHILL, SLICE, AND SERVE

Transfer to the fridge to cool completely. Once the chocolate is set, slice the cake into pieces and serve.

TIP – To crush the graham crackers, put them in a plastic bag and smash with a rolling pin. Don't break them too finely, though—you want the cake to have plenty of texture.

PLAN OF ACTION! ❶ MELT CHOCOLATE MIXTURE → ❷ ADD DRY INGREDIENTS → ❸ CHILL, SLICE, AND SERVE

CHOCOLATE CHIP COOKIES

PLAN OF ACTION!

These easy-to-make cookies are soft and chewy, and incredibly delicious. Double the recipe if you're having friends over, then serve with a glass of milk for the perfect afternoon treat!

MAKES 15 • **READY IN** 20 mins, plus cooling

1 CREAM THE BUTTER AND SUGARS

Preheat the oven to 350°F (180°C). In a large bowl, cream together the butter and sugars with an electric hand-held mixer until light and fluffy. Beat in the egg and vanilla extract.

2 ADD THE FLOUR AND CHOCOLATE CHIPS

Sift together the flour, baking powder, and salt and mix into the wet mixture until well-combined. Fold in the chocolate chips.

3 SPOON OUT THE MIX

Place tablespoons of the cookie mixture onto several baking sheets, making sure that they are spaced well apart as they will spread while cooking.

4 BAKE AND COOL

Bake the cookies in the middle of the oven for 13–15 minutes, until they are lightly colored and just cooked. Let the cookies cool on the baking sheets for 5 minutes before transferring to a wire rack to cool completely. Serve with a glass of milk.

For lots more quick cookie recipe ideas and variations, see pp240–41.

| 1 CREAM BUTTER | → | 2 ADD FLOUR | → | 3 SPOON OUT MIX | → | 4 BAKE AND COOL |

INGREDIENTS

7 tbsp unsalted butter, softened

½ cup granulated sugar

½ cup light brown sugar

1 large egg

1 tsp vanilla extract

1 cup all-purpose flour

½ tsp baking powder

½ tsp salt

3½oz (100g) milk chocolate chips

COOKIE JAR

BUTTERSCOTCH AND MARSHMALLOW COOKIES

Add ½ cup each of butterscotch chunks and mini marshmallows to the basic dough, then bake.

THUMBPRINT COOKIES

Divide the basic dough into 15 pieces, roll each piece into a ball, flatten it out, and press your thumb into the center. Fill each "thumbprint" with 1 tsp raspberry jam (or jam of your choice), then bake.

CHOCOLATE AND CHERRY COOKIES

Add ¼ cup cocoa powder, 1 tbsp brown sugar, 3½oz (100g) each of chocolate chunks and dried cherries, and 1 tsp vanilla to the basic dough, then bake.

PEANUT BUTTER COOKIES

Add ¼ cup peanut butter, 1 tsp vanilla extract, and ¼ cup crushed peanuts to the basic dough, then bake.

- - - - Don't worry if you get caught with your hand in the cookie jar—you deserve a treat, after all! For these scrumptious recipes, follow the basic cookie dough method and baking instructions on pages 238–40 (omitting the chocolate chips), adapt as below, and divide into 15 equal pieces.

OATMEAL AND RAISIN COOKIES

Add ½ cup each of oatmeal and raisins, 1 tbsp brown sugar, and 1 tsp vanilla extract to the basic dough, then bake.

ZESTY LIME COOKIES

Mix 1 tbsp grated lime zest and the juice of 1 lime into the basic dough, then bake.

WHITE CHOC AND MACADAMIA NUT COOKIES

Add 3½oz (100g) each of white chocolate chunks and chopped macadamia nuts, and 1 tsp vanilla extract to the basic dough, then bake.

SNICKERDOODLES

Mix together ½ cup sugar, 1 tsp salt, and 2 tbsp ground cinnamon. Divide the basic dough into 15 pieces, roll each piece into a ball, then roll each ball in the sugar and cinnamon mix to coat. Flatten slightly before baking.

QUICK BROWNIES

Soft and moist in the center and crisp on top, these classic brownies are so easy to prepare. You can store them for up to 3 days in an airtight container.

MAKES 24 • **READY IN** 20–30 mins, plus cooling
SPECIAL EQUIPMENT 9 x 12in (23 x 30cm) brownie pan, or similar

- 12 tbsp unsalted butter, diced
- 10oz (300g) good-quality dark chocolate, broken into pieces
- 10oz (300g) granulated sugar
- 4 large eggs, beaten
- 1¼ cups all-purpose flour
- ¼ cup cocoa powder, plus extra for dusting

MAKE THE BATTER

1 MELT

butter
chocolate
WOODEN SPOON
HEATPROOF BOWL
SAUCEPAN

Melt the butter and chocolate in a bowl over a pan of simmering water. Let cool. Preheat the oven to 400°F (200°C).

2 COMBINE

sugar
beaten eggs

Add the sugar and mix well. Then add the eggs, a little at a time, and combine.

3 SIFT AND MIX

flour and cocoa powder
SIEVE

Sift in the flour and cocoa powder. Mix until smooth.

FORM AND BAKE

4 SPREAD

batter

PARCHMENT PAPER

SPATULA

BROWNIE PAN

Line the pan with parchment. Some should hang over the sides. Pour in the batter and spread it out evenly.

Bake for 12–15 minutes, until firm to the touch and a skewer inserted comes out coated with a little batter. Cool completely.

METAL SKEWER

5 BAKE

LIFT THE BROWNIE FROM THE PAN AND SCORE THE SURFACE INTO 24 PIECES.

SLICE AND SERVE

6 SLICE

SHARP KNIFE

hot water

Slice the brownie along the score lines, wiping the knife and dipping it in hot water between cuts.

7 DUST

cocoa powder

SIEVE

Sift cocoa powder over and serve.

SOUR CHERRY AND CHOCOLATE BROWNIES

For a quick yet decadent dessert, try these gooey, fudge-style brownies. The sharp and chewy dried sour cherries contrast wonderfully with the rich, dark chocolate.

MAKES 16 • **READY IN 20–30 mins, plus cooling**
SPECIAL EQUIPMENT 8 x 10in (20 x 25cm) brownie pan or similar

INGREDIENTS

- 11 tbsp unsalted butter, diced, plus extra for greasing
- 5½oz (150g) good-quality dark chocolate, broken into pieces
- 1 cup light brown sugar
- 3 eggs
- 1 tsp vanilla extract
- 1¼ cup self-rising flour, sifted
- 3½oz (100g) dried sour cherries
- 3½oz (100g) dark chocolate chunks

❶ PREPARE THE PAN

Preheat the oven to 400°F (200°C). Grease the brownie pan and line with parchment paper, allowing for some overhang.

❷ MAKE THE BATTER

Melt the butter and chocolate in a heatproof bowl over a saucepan of simmering water (make sure the bowl doesn't touch the water as the chocolate may burn). Remove from the heat, add the sugar, and stir to combine. Cool slightly, add the eggs and vanilla extract, and mix to combine. Add the flour and fold it in gently, being careful not to over-mix. Fold in the sour cherries and chocolate chunks.

❸ POUR AND BAKE

Pour the batter into the prepared pan and gently spread it out into the corners. Bake in the center of the oven for 12–15 minutes, or until just firm to the touch on top but still soft underneath.

❹ COOL AND STORE

Let the brownie cool in the pan for 5 minutes. Then turn out and cut into squares. Place on a wire rack to cool completely, then serve or store for up to 3 days.

PLAN OF ACTION! → ❶ PREPARE PAN → ❷ MAKE BATTER → ❸ POUR AND BAKE → ❹ COOL AND STORE

WHITE CHOCOLATE AND MACADAMIA NUT BLONDIES

Blondies are simply white chocolate versions of brownies. The macadamia nuts here add a buttery crunch to these moist treats—a perfect match for the creamy white chocolate.

MAKES 24 • **READY IN** 20–30 mins, plus cooling
SPECIAL EQUIPMENT 8 x 10in (20 x 25cm) brownie pan or similar

INGREDIENTS

- 12 tbsp unsalted butter, diced, plus extra for greasing
- 10oz (300g) white chocolate, broken into pieces
- 1¼ cups granulated sugar
- 4 large eggs
- 1½ cups all-purpose flour, sifted
- 3½oz (100g) macadamia nuts, roughly chopped

① PREPARE THE PAN
Preheat the oven to 400°F (200°C). Grease the brownie pan and line with parchment paper, allowing for some overhang.

② MAKE THE BATTER
Melt the butter and chocolate in a heatproof bowl over a saucepan of simmering water (make sure the bowl doesn't touch the water as the chocolate may burn). Remove, and let cool for 20 minutes. Then add the sugar and mix well to combine. Using a balloon whisk, beat in the eggs, one at a time, until well incorporated. Then fold in the flour and stir in the nuts.

③ POUR AND BAKE
Pour the batter into the prepared pan and gently spread it out into the corners. Bake for 12–15 minutes, or until just firm to the touch on top but still soft underneath.

④ COOL AND STORE
Let cool completely in the pan, then cut into 24 squares and serve or store for up to 5 days.

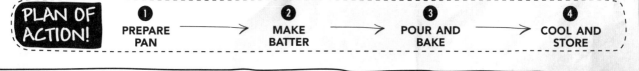

PLAN OF ACTION!
① PREPARE PAN → ② MAKE BATTER → ③ POUR AND BAKE → ④ COOL AND STORE

INGREDIENTS

3 tbsp butter, softened, plus extra for greasing

9oz (250g) dark chocolate, chopped

½ cup superfine sugar

4 eggs

½ tsp pure vanilla extract

¼ cup all-purpose flour

pinch of salt

whipped cream, vanilla ice cream, or hot custard flavored with orange zest, to serve (optional)

MOLTEN CHOCOLATE CAKES

A delight for all chocoholics, these easy-to-make treats have a light cake surrounding a rich, creamy chocolate center. Add a scoop or two of vanilla ice cream and you've got a simple and speedy decadent dessert.

SERVES 4 • **READY IN** 20 mins
SPECIAL EQUIPMENT Four 6fl oz (175ml) ramekins

1 PREPARE THE RAMEKINS

Generously butter the sides and bottom of the ramekins. Cut a piece of parchment paper to fit in the bottom of each and put in position. Set aside. Preheat the oven to 400°F (200°C).

2 MELT THE CHOCOLATE

Put the chocolate in a heatproof bowl set over a pan of simmering water, without letting the bowl touch the water, and stir for 5 minutes, or until the chocolate is melted and smooth. Set aside.

3 MAKE THE BATTER

While the chocolate is melting, beat the butter and sugar with an electric mixer until blended and smooth. Beat in the eggs one at a time, beating well after each addition, then add the vanilla. Sift the flour and salt together and gently stir in, then stir in the chocolate. Divide the batter equally between the ramekins: the mixture won't fill them to the tops.

4 BAKE THE CAKES

Place the ramekins on a baking sheet and bake for 12–15 minutes, or until the sides are set but the centers are still soft when lightly pressed with your fingertips.

5 INVERT AND SERVE

Put an individual serving plate on top of each cake, then, wearing oven mitts, invert both so the cake sits on the serving plate. Remove the lining paper. Serve the cakes hot, with softly whipped cream, vanilla ice cream, or hot custard flavored with orange zest if desired.

TIP – Coarsely chop leftovers and spoon them over vanilla ice cream with hot fudge sauce to make a delicious sundae (see pp220–21 for more sundae ideas).

Try using some of the more exotically flavored dark chocolate available—such as cardamom and orange, or chile-flavored chocolate.

INDEX

Entries in **bold** indicate ingredients.

M

macadamia nuts: white chocolate and
macadamia nut blondies 245
white chocolate and macadamia nut
cookies 241
mackerel: herbed mackerel salad 114–15
smoked mackerel roll 105
mangoes: diced mango and avocado
bruschetta 181
mango and lime dressing 91
mango and shrimp salad 89
mango salsa 146
pineapple and mango fresh fruit hand
pies 234
maple syrup: cornmeal waffles with bacon
maple sauce 49
maple syrup, cinnamon, and apple
oatmeal 28
margherita in minutes 152–3
marshmallows: butterscotch and
marshmallow cookies 240
marshmallow and banana split
sundae 221
mascarpone cheese: mascarpone,
peaches, honey, and mint pancake
topping 44
raspberry cheesecake 226–7
mayonnaise, lemon, and basil 71
meatballs, Thai-spiced 122
Mediterranean mix one-pot meals 134
meringues: Eton mess with warm fruit
coulis 224–5
Mexican green rice 111
milkshakes 222
mint: mint pesto 136
minty yogurt dressing 91
summer pea, mint, and quinoa soup 86
molten chocolate cakes 246–7
Moroccan-style shrimp 171
moules marinières 192–3
muffins: banana and oat bran 34–5
lemon and poppy seed 36
quinoa and polenta 37
mushrooms: balsamic mushrooms with
cream cheese bruschetta 180

beef stroganoff 151
chicken, red and yellow bell pepper,
mushroom, and bacon skewers 199
Portobello mushrooms and feta with
spinach, red onion, and olive pita
pockets 78
Portobello mushrooms filled with
pesto, mozzarella, and tomato 132
spinach and mushrooms quiche cups 187
mussels: moules marinières 192–3
mustard: honey mustard dipping sauce 200

N

Neapolitan float 223
noodles: Asian noodle salad 88
dan dan noodles 123
green papaya, beef, and noodle salad
96–7
pad Thai 128–9
stir-fries 124
nori: do-it-yourself sushi 104–5
nutty blue smoothie 25

O

oat bran: banana and oat bran muffins 34–5
oatmeal: oatmeal and raisin
cookies 241
oats: granola blends 32
overnight oats 29
perfect oatmeal 28
quick stovetop granola 30–31
oils 13, 32
salad dressings 90
olives 15
charcuterie board accompaniment 188
citrus-marinated 164
pan bagna 66–7
pizza topping 154
smart shopping
tapenade 167
omelets: cheese soufflé 56–7
classic 54–5
one-pot meals 134–5
onions: dicing 16–17
pickled 174, 188
potato, pancetta, and red onion hash
62–3
tomato, mozzarella, and red onion
salad 93
oranges: fresh oranges with caramel and
passion fruit 210–11
orange sorbet 216–17

P

pad Thai 128–9
pan bagna 66–7
pancakes: blueberry 46–7
buttermilk 42–3
caramelized apple and chocolate
crêpes 231
toppings 44–5
pancetta: pea and pancetta pasta 140–41
potato, pancetta, and red onion hash
62–3
sautéed scallops with pancetta 191
panna cotta 230
panzanella 110
papaya: green papaya, beef, and noodle
salad 96–7
passion fruit, fresh oranges with caramel
and 210–11
pasta: broccoli and blue cheese pasta
sauce 138
Caprese pasta salad 89
one-pot pasta 135
pea and pancetta pasta 140–41
smoked salmon and crème fraîche
spaghetti 190
tuna and artichoke salad 102–3
pastry: fresh fruit hand pies 234–5
quiche cups 187
peaches: almond and peach overnight
oats 29
dreamy peach smoothie 25
mascarpone, peaches, and honey with
fresh mint leaves pancake topping 44
peach and ginger fresh fruit hand pies
234
peach salsa 146
plain yogurt, peach slices, and honey
toast topping 39
scallops, peach, and red onion skewers
198
vanilla and peach oatmeal 28
peanut butter: banana and peanut butter
shake 222
chocolate and peanut butter pretzel
sundae 220
peanut and lime dip 201
peanut butter, banana, crushed walnut,
cinnamon, and honey toast

ACKNOWLEDGMENTS

ABOUT THE AUTHOR

Elena Rosemond-Hoerr is the coauthor of DK's *The American Cookbook* and contributor to DK's *The Meat Cookbook*. She is a writer, photographer, and author of the award-winning food blog biscuitsandsuch.com. Between developing recipes and writing cookbooks, Elena has a lot of experience fitting quick meals into a busy schedule.

ABOUT THE CONTRIBUTOR

Laura Herring has worked as a writer and cookbook editor for multiple publishers for more than 10 years.

She has worked with many top chefs from around the world on books covering almost every type of cooking from pies to paella to four-tier party cakes. Always in a hurry but never wanting to miss a meal, this is the perfect book for her. She currently lives in London.

ELENA ROSEMOND-HOERR WOULD LIKE TO THANK

Dan for his support and love.

DK WOULD LIKE TO THANK

Stuart West for new recipe photography; William Reavell for additional photography; Geoff Fennell for photography art direction; Kate Wesson and Jane Lawrie for food styling; Isabel de Cordova for prop styling; Bob Saxton, Kathy Woolley, and Neha Samuel for editorial assistance; Mandy Earey and Hannah Moore for design assistance; Claire Cross and Jackie Hornberger for proofreading; and Vanessa Bird for the index.

All photography and artworks © Dorling Kindersley
For further information see: **www.dkimages.com**